BEWARE OF THE ALMIGHTY

Destiny of the doG

VIE Loriot de Rouvray

Printed in the United States of America

ISBN: 979-8-9897845-2-3(Paperback)
ISBN: 979-8-9897845-3-0 (Hardback)
ISBN: 979-8-9897845-4-7   (eBook)

There was an old owl. The more he listened, the wiser he got.

—CHADD, ghost writer

Faith heals the invisible, believes the incredible, and receives the impossible.

—Jesus

Contents

Prologue

This book is fictitious to bring real and true powerful messages of the plot of a few hundred of the richest Reptilians that control the planet, with their bloodlines of Archons—fallen angels mixed with human beings—that act as their minions. They are cold-blooded with no sympathy or compassion.

It is built upon insight while times of political corruption and financial instability are growing, launching a spiritual adventure that will transform all who take the journey. Intense power of synchro-nicity and spiritual purpose that is blending the adventure to the real insight and visions that the characters encounter. With a curse that has been put as obstacles to the couple called the God Duo Warriors—CHADD and VIE.

I have been guided to deliver messages through this story, as the Archons, which are of Reptilians bloodlines and that are working for them, have set some thought form of limitation in place because they do not like the idea that they have to leave earth.

They have called themselves the New World Order.

Some of these entities have attached themselves to some people's aura or gotten into their body to get information from these persons. It is to enable these people at the same time to get clarity of thought.

These Reptilians bloodlines seek their information from the entities they have attached to and then deliver it in a twisted manner, but they also make human beings do unwilling and uncontrolled evil acts—shootings at schools, shootings of families for no reason, priests that abuse children. Also, killing children that are the future and are born with a different DNA and are knowledgeable—these children came to help us.

These individuals with dark energy are actually in top key places such as banks, governments, school systems, churches, the Vatican, medical systems, the media, and secret societies.

Blood is the most potent multidimensional connection in our bodies. It is what is at stake in this battle. It is the holy blood or Holy Grail.

Various and many sources on our planet are attempting to convince humans to fear the ascension and the end of the Mayan calendar. And they have imprinted fear and scarcity into human beings' minds that fear the worst and even think that all species will die.

All that is coming is the removal of their control. At the end of the Mayan calendar, the solar system, Archons and Maya will simply merge in the photon band with us.

I did not know that in writing this book, I would be entering a period of a three-year journey of fights against fourth-dimensional dark energies.

First I had to fight a woman that made me lose nine months and money, then a man that offered his help with this book and got lost in his journey in the middle of it and became an obstacle to the edition—he made me lose, again, over a year of time. Many others tried to trick me, like the dark mentalist energy that was given to my relatives, some very nasty, twisted information about me and that have tried to have me put on psychiatric drugs.

Synopsis

While at her favorite place, VIE encounters a person in a wheelchair by the name of CHADD. Immediately she feels a deep and strong connection that she cannot explain. CHADD and VIE have lived together in previous lives, and VIE begins to have visions of the past they had together. Her memory is awakening as she gets back to the past during her sleep, and she continues to live her life.

As she gets to know him better, she becomes enveloped in a world of mysticism, government conspiracies, religions, and upcoming prophesied events. VIE is not prepared for such life-changing experiences in a world she never has known before. How is she to know that her world would all change because of that day when she went for a cup of coffee and a good book to read? That day, she was entering a world of lies, deception, hope, and pain. Her spiritual journey is about to begin when VIE joins forces with her blue flame, CHADD, to bring the words of Jesus to those that are question-ing what will happen to them when the Mayan calendar ends and beyond.

The alternative training that VIE received by the Archangel Michael suddenly makes sense; it prepared her to look beyond the veil of what she could only see with her eyes. She can now see with her mind and her heart. All of her experiences prepared VIE for what was to come.

Summary

Henri lived in Montana growing up. He lived near an Indian tribal reservation. He would hear stories and legends of black caves that were filled with treasures. Over time, with deforestation and earthquakes that ravaged the land, the caves disappeared. The Indians believed that the caves were a holy place and protected them in keeping the lands as a reservation. They also believe that the Indian Christ left a holy medallion in one of the caves before he went to heaven.

The day before he was getting ready to leave for Canada, he heard, "Seek and you shall find."

Henri went to the area that the legend of the black caves spoke about. As he looked, he found a small opening in one side of the mountain. As he climbed into the opening, it began to sparkle when his lamp shone upon it. He wandered down the chasm. He lit a match and then saw a black medallion. He took the black medallion with him home. On his way back home, he noticed some writing on it that was in a different language. He had heard that Christ said that the medallion came from a cosmic place and the beginning of time. He quickly buried it in the corner of his family barn and left the following day. Henri's journey took him to Europe, to college, as a professor, to digging sites, and later as an OSS operative.

At Antioch, a merchant invited him into his house and gave him as a present another medallion that looked very similar to the one he had found years before.

Henri got married and came back to the USA. He went to ask his friend at the museum what the writing meant. People at the museum told him that it was a form of Hebrew and advised him to contact a person in Jerusalem. Before he did that, he returned home with his wife, Martha, and his newborn son, Edward, to meet his parents in Montana. Then he went to show the medallions to his friend, the chief of the Indian reservation. The Indian chief looked with great attention to the medallion and told him, "You are the beginning, but he is not the end."

He gave his son the medallion from Antioch, and years later he dug up the other one that he buried earlier.

Edward had exceptional intelligence. He finished high school at the age of fourteen, college at sixteen, and then became a lawyer. He joined a secret political group at college. He was contacted by NSA to work for the government. His personality and disposition changed completely the day he began to wear the medallion.

His mother Martha placed the medallion over the crib, and Edward would often hit the medallion with his little feet and play with it. As if he knew that this would keep activating it.

Edward had a hereditary purple birthmark on his finger. It was passed from generation to generation, on his father's side, to each son in the family.

Edward married a girl named Ethel, and they had a son named CHADD. (Edward divorced later on to remarry Katherine.)

The DNA had changed in Edward, CHADD's father, by the medallion. Henri gave this medallion to Ethel for CHADD, his grandson, and she, too, placed it over his crib for CHADD to play with. CHADD was very drawn to the medallion when he received it when he turned eighteen.

Henri had contacted several people in his attempt to decipher the writings and age of both medallions. He heard only that the writ-ing on it was placed there over three thousand years ago. The writing surpassed the writings found at Khirbet Qeiyafa, but to complicate things even more, the material was not of earthly origin. It seemed to have come from either a comet or some other means from the sky. Carbon dating cannot date things over sixty thousand years old, and at one time, they needed to be alive. The age could not be accurately determined by carbon dating or by argon-argon testing because of the material.

Henri started having strange dreams about CHADD and his safety when CHADD was around twelve. He went to see his Indian brother Golden Eagle about these dreams. He was told that he and his wife's lives were in danger. And that the medallion that he found in the mountains needed to be protected at all cost.

Shortly after the warning, Henri and Martha were poisoned by the drinking water at their Montana home. Someone had poisoned the well at their home.

CHADD had been diagnosed with several behavior and mental problems over the years. Ironically though, he was never sick. His father, Edward, and his mother, Ethel, took him for all kinds of evaluations. Even though his behavioral issues were diagnosed with classical definitions, his IQ was way off the charts. CHADD also had the same birthmark on his left ring finger as the other men in his family. He became of interest to his father's employers partly because of Edward's concerns of CHADD's behavior but also because of his brilliance. CHADD had been taken to the government hospital that his father used at the request of the NSA. As a young boy at the age of five, they started to do testing on CHADD to understand his unique abilities.

They found that his DNA had been altered, and they didn't know why. They didn't understand that the medallions were only tuned to Henri's, Edward's, and CHADD's vibrations—much like a satellite, TV transponder frequency, and a satellite TV receiver. The signal has to be received, understood, have signal strength, and then approved for viewing. It seemed a higher intelligence was allowing all of this to happen to CHADD.

CHADD was then given multiple drugs starting at the age of five. His mother, Ethel, could not tolerate her son being given drugs at such a young age. That and Edward's immense code of security were the main reasons that she and Edward divorced. She started taking pharmaceutical drugs for her own depression and anxiety, at Edward's coaching and the doctor's urging (government hospital). She soon became addicted to prescription drugs, and her behavior became more and more erratic. When Edward and Ethel went to court for their divorce, Edward depicted Ethel as an unfit mother and a drug addict to the court, and the court awarded custody to his father. During the time of Edward and Ethel's separation, he started dating a coworker named Katherine. Ethel would later find out that he was having an affair with her as far back as when she was pregnant with CHADD.

Ethel found a place very close to where CHADD lived and had typical visitation rights and shared in parental decisions that concerned medical treatment and education. She could see how the drugs were affecting her young son. She complained to Edward. At first he seemed to be sympathetic, but then he married Katherine and things changed. Edward became more and more distant from Ethel, and the willingness to discuss CHADD became less and less import-ant. CHADD was also having a hard time coping with Katherine's son, Paul, who was about the same age as CHADD. Katherine tried to alienate Ethel and CHADD as much as she could over the years. She wouldn't let CHADD talk to his mom on the phone, wouldn't have him ready for visitation, tell him that his mother stole his col-lege addict. This weighed heavily on Ethel's mind daily.

As time went on, Ethel became increasingly dependent on her medications. The doctor she was seeing also worked for the NSA. He was working with Edward's group too. She became more withdrawn, and CHADD was becoming more difficult to be around as he grew older.

The day came when CHADD was twelve and visiting his mom. He was especially out of control and told his mom, "I'm going to kill myself. I can't take this anymore."

Ethel immediately called Edward and told him that he needed to have him evaluated. Edward came directly to the house, picked up CHADD, and took him to the regular doctor and had him eval-uated. Eventually, CHADD was put in a US behavior center in California. He spent two years there. She would see him every two months and could speak to him once a week. It was costing Edward $6,000 a month, which Katherine did not like. She found another center called Punta Cayenna. She talked Edward into bringing him back to South Florida for a short stay before Edward told CHADD they were going on a vacation to Punta Cayenna. When they arrived in Punta Cayenna, Edward and CHADD left to go look at another "school." After they arrived, CHADD was left at the new school, betrayed again by his father.

Ethel was furious when she found out that CHADD was left at the school. She had tried calling Edward on his cell phone and the house phone but had no response. Edward eventually told her that they had gone on vacation in Punta Cayenna and that he had found a behavior center in Punta Cayenna that was better suited for CHADD's issue. Because Edward had primary custody and Katherine was jealous of Ethel, the center had been told that Ethel should not call or see him because she would be detrimental to his treatment.

Ethel found out that in Punta Cayenna, the patient becomes the custody of the state and she could not see him without the center's consent. She also could not remove him from the center called Punta Cayenna without approval of the state. Punta Cayenna is located on the southern coast of Punta Cayenna.

CHADD had met many different types of boys at the bay. Some were drug dealers, drug addicts, violent offenders, cutters, and rapists. He was different. He was not a criminal.

His only crimes were that he was moody, depressed, argumentative, oppositional, and defiant. He always kept his honor, but he lost his belief in God. Ethel went to the center three months after he was left there but was monitored by the guards. He saw his mother every six months, and he was allowed a phone call from his mother once a month. Ethel went to the bay three months after he went there but was monitored by the guards. No air conditioning, food with bugs in it, physical abuse. These and other abusive conditions were found by Ethel. That was the time that Ethel decided to continue with legal action.

Ethel immediately contacted her attorney about her rights, but she fought a losing battle. Edward knew everyone in the legal system in South Florida. They all were members of the same organizations and clubs. Edward had special considerations working for the NSA. Ethel did everything she could to get CHADD back into the USA, but Edward worked the system and left Ethel penniless and having to file bankruptcy. The stress on Ethel's fragile emotional state created more issues for her. After four years of legal battles, the case was finally judged to be in favor of Edward. The case was decided by a judge, not a jury, and the attorney who was supposed to protect CHADD also had connections to the NSA. After that battle, Ethel had no more fight in her. She did all she could for CHADD, but it was not enough.

The day after the court found in Edward's favor, Edward decided to bring CHADD back to the States and put him in a behav-ior center in Mississippi. At this point, Ethel could hardly function. CHADD was at the behavior center in Mississippi a month before he turned eighteen and moved in with his mother. He would still see and talk to his father; he was still looking for approval from him. Katherine didn't want him staying at the house. She didn't want any-thing to do with him and would make up stories to influence Edward in a negative way. She wanted all the praise to go to her golden child Paul and for Edward to treat him like his only son. She did, however, keep very close tabs on him and what he was doing.

CHADD began wearing his medallion when he turned eigh-teen, as Henri had requested of Ethel. CHADD didn't have an edu-cation or social skills since he was locked up at the centers for eight years, but he was a quick learner. He had lots of anger. One day when seeing his stepbrother, Paul, a deputy sheriff, Paul mentioned to CHADD that they had a program at the department for confiden-tial informers. CHADD jumped at the opportunity. One day he met his old friend Marco from the center, who was once again dealing drugs. Marco told him his father was sending him into the federal building in Miami to buy drugs from the government. CHADD didn't believe him. Marco came to CHADD one afternoon and told him a new person had made the drop. He had the same type of medallion as CHADD. CHADD asked him what the new person looked like and his name. Marco told him what he looked like and his name was Mr. E. CHADD immediately made the connection. It was his father who worked in that building in Miami and had the same type of medallion.

CHADD saw his chance to pay back his father for taking away his childhood. He went to his father's house and hacked into his father's computer when Edward and Katherine were gone. He down-loaded as much information as he could and made two copies.

When he and Edward were alone, CHADD told him what he was doing and what he had discovered as well as Marco's experiences. CHADD told his father that he knew that his father was involved with drugs from money by the government. The government would take the drugs from drug dealers out west, send them to Miami for sale in Florida, and generate money to the government's clandes-tine operations—black ops. CHADD wanted money, lots of money for his silence. His father would pay for what he did. Edward told CHADD to go home and that he would find a way to give him the money he wanted.

That put everything into motion. Edward called his people at the NSA, and they told Edward that they would have to silence CHADD. Edward told them that he understood, but he was a valu-able asset because of his intelligence and his uniqueness. They agreed to commit him, use him, and keep him alive by drugging him for future use. CHADD was picked up and taken to the hospital. Marco and everyone connected with him were killed. No one would ques-tion the deaths of drug dealers.

CHADD spent time in hospitals and medical centers. The gov-ernment knew of his uniqueness by doing DNA testing at the center in Punta Cayenna. Paul had been watching him at the department and knew everything he was doing.

It was in the hospital that his beliefs changed. He was under mind-altering drugs, had several near-death experiences, and could channel messages from the other side. He was now filled with love and the knowledge that God does exist. He also knew that his life had a purpose, but the purpose could not be completed unless there was a uniting and reuniting of things in his life. During his stay in the hospital, a group called the Guardians revealed themselves.

They had existed throughout history. They were the Cathari. There were two elements to them—the Perfecti and the Believers. They had existed in many places in history. The Perfecti were the helpful ones and wanted to bring people closer to God. They helped defeat Hitler, protected innocent women and children, and then disappeared into another time. The Believers were the Nazis that escaped to South America, never to be found, the members of many civilizations that killed women and children. They are the serial killers of today and many world leaders that destroyed rather than created. The Perfecti were the da Vincis, Mother Theresas, and Mozarts of yesterday and today. They went to war with each other when the Pope sent the troops to slaughter them and their women and children. The Believers were willing to live off the world but now wanted revenge against humanity for what was done against them.

The two factions were always in battle with one another. They could destroy each other, but there were more born every day. They looked completely human but did have the rather unique upper brow that would set them apart. Extremely intelligent and hypnotiz-ing at the same time, some of the Believers had guidance in genetic reproduction thousands of years ago, before and after the great flood, to create creatures seen throughout history as vampires, werewolves, Bigfoot, and reptilians. The Cathari were the descendants of the angels in the book of Enoch that mated with earthly women. Some took on virtues of love and kindness (Perfecti), and others took on the love of money, power, pain, and destruction (Believers). The duality was always there during battle and had existed since the angels came down to earth.

CHADD then met VIE. Their meeting set things in motion for 2012 and the coming of Christ. There have been many battles between the God of Good and the God of Evil. CHADD is constantly under drugs, and Edward and Katherine have full guardianship over CHADD. His father and his wife must approve every move he makes.

During this time, Ethel is getting very sick, she is on all kinds of drugs, and her condition is deteriorating. CHADD tells his mom what is going on, but she is helpless and not strong enough to help him. VIE starts to spend time with her to try to find out more about CHADD.

Ethel tells VIE that she can't do it alone. If VIE would help her, she would expose the government involvement with her son, CHADD. The next morning, when VIE went to pick up Ethel, she found her with an apparent drug overdose, but what was the truth?

VIE knows her time is next; she can channel to the other side. She is guided to protect CHADD and bring him to their true purpose.

The NSA feels that too many people now know about their involvement with their operations, the Cathari and CHADD. Edward returned home and overheard Katherine speaking to Paul that the NSA wanted him to protect the Believers as they kill CHADD and VIE. Katherine was told that the NSA had gotten all they needed from CHADD, particularly his DNA, to clone with the Believers to create a super race. He also had seen Katherine at their build-ing with President Russell Mundi. Putting two and two together, he realized that he was Rex Mundi—the God of Evil. He also realized that the NSA and the Believers always manipulated Katherine. She was the one that found the center on the island of Punta Cayenna for CHADD. She had tried to split them apart, had joint guardian-ship, supported CHADD's prescription drug use almost his entire life, and, now that they considered his usefulness over, his untimely death. He finds out that they also killed Ethel and that Katherine never loved him. It was a scam.

Edward realized that he was always played for a fool. He had to save his son before it is too late.

Definitions

For the conspiracy theory thriller:

Vajra—lightning, diamond-like. Means "the hand and mighty me." The purpose of this emblem is to awaken human beings. Very powerful.

Ankh—means VIE (life), union of heaven and earth, oneness.

VIE—door to the divine, the Chosen One.

Eagle—power, authority, truth. It is the ultimate solar symbol. Means "ray of light."

CHADD (tainted angel)—the eagle, ultimate solar symbol, and blue flame ray of light. Is protected and counter-balanced by his loving dove, VIE. And when he is finally united with his dove, guided by the Ruby, becomes royalty. They are now the two royal eagles connected by the heart and the two missionar-ies (God Duo) can make their nest. CHADD is an eagle blue ray. It represents divine inspiration. Emblem of emperors and empires. An eagle is able to detect atmospheric charges that can herald a storm or earthquake up to ten hours before it strikes.

Albatross—Messenger of GOD.

Dove—associated with feminine love and peace. Dove is the secret, covert bird symbol of the USA. The dove (soft and reasonable) is counterbalancing the masculine glory of the eagle. "VIE balances her eagle."

Ruby—system of royalty and symbol of protection. VIE is also the aristocrat. Ruby from Louis XIV called Roi Soleil: RA. One ruby had been placed on the roof of the temple of the Holy Grail so that the Grail knights could be guided toward it in the dark. *For health*: place one ruby on the left side of the body in such a way that it touches the skin, and it protects the wearer from ill health. The ruby color connects to the heart and circu-latory system.

Reptilians—these are creatures that are nonhuman that can shape-shift. This means that they can alter their DNA electrically to transform from a human form to one that is reptilian. They have to concentrate to keep their human shape; if not, they turn into reptilian humanoid. It appears that when reptilians get very angry, they lose their human cover and turn into reptil-ian humanoids. See shapeshifters caught on film at http://www. stargods.org/ClintonShapeShift.htm, etc.

Archons/Jens—Reptilian bloodlines.

The Vow of Christ

As she stared into his eyes, she felt calmness entering her being. She watched as eternity unfolded within her. She saw the creation of matter in the beginning when they had walked in paradise, before the evil one had placed the curse on them. She felt their innocence and rejoiced in her memory of when death did not exist and life was eternally known. She beheld the radiance of their light when it lived in the kingdom of the forgotten God, and for a brief moment, she felt bliss.

Breaking his gaze, he said, "Go now before they see you, and remember, I shall not leave you in darkness but shall place my light around you until my return."

Caressing his face, she said, "My husband of spirit and Lord of Light, may you rest in the bosom of the forgotten God, and may he hear my plea and return you back to me when we are ready to experience our love again in the world of form."

One "Victorious in Christ"

The earth of Christ is a light and vibrational grid matrix, and it holds the energetic blueprint of all life on this earth, keeping the earth in existence.

The equality of the feminine and the masculine is part of Jesus's teachings withheld by the Church along with the pure soul of Mary Magdalene.

After two thousand years, Mary Magdalene has to be celebrated for who she really is, true divine loveliness and a goddess! Mary Magdalene and Jesus are coming from the universe to help humanity and Mother Earth in her ascension.

When Jesus was on earth years ago, he carried a specific DNA throughout his physical body, as did his parents.

Jesus and Mary Magdalene were married, and they had children together.

Jesus's DNA and also His spouse's DNA, which was the same as his parents, was available to be inherited by their three children.

Preface

I wrote this book to explain my work and my mission. My mission is to help you become your own master, reconnect you to your higher self, and to raise your vibration. You will be guided on your path to your purpose and destiny.

My alternative work is a gift for you, guided by my spiritual family of angels. I am blessed with the Christ consciousness following eighteen months of daily initiation and preparation from Archangel Michael. The gift clears and raises your vibration along with restoring your intimate connection to the Divine, from which you have been disconnected. Connection may be achieved through CHADD or me.

As the energy of the earth is changing, pharmaceutical drugs will have no effect on people. I have added a lot of information on various alternative therapies so that it may help you see the world around you more clearly. I have been blessed with a gift from God as a light worker, which means that I work with Light and Sound and Sacred Geometric forms. I am also helped by my blue flame on this side along with the cosmic doctors and Nikola Tesla on the other side. It is a joy, a pleasure, and an honor to help and prepare you for an essential three-step process necessary for the ascension and beyond it. I have a different energy and knowledge that was given to me directly from God, which clears and raises your vibration and will restore your intimate connection with the Divine in preparation for the end of this cycle. By awakening your light body, you will be guided on your path to your purpose and toward your destiny.

There are three very important steps to achieve that preparation:

1. You must acknowledge your Creator, Jesus.
2. Clear your karmic past, your emotions stuck from your past.
3. Rejuvenate the physical body.

I am willing to share the information in this book with you knowing it will be a great help to you and your children very soon.

Introduction

I have been chosen. I am the door to the Divine. I have lived many lives before this one, but I have come back to help you and to accomplish a mission that is to help you become your own master.

This book is dedicated to bringing powerful messages to the world. With warnings and future predictions that you may not want to hear.

This book is about hope, courage, and freedom.

Prophecies fulfilled.

A battle of evil and good.

The matrix and the ascension process.

My name is VIE. I am your guide into the light and into the darkness as I remember them.

I can raise your vibration and reconnect your DNA through different ways of using my light energy using the sound frequency of my voice and the language of the light, by sending you energy from my heart center in quantum, etc. It is then aligning you to your path in awakening its memory by unlocking the program.

I am the first Aquarius to come with a knowledge that will take humanity a little more than two thousand years to integrate.

I was led to remember who I was on the other side of the veil, for what purpose and what gifts I was coming back on earth with. Also to reconnect with my blue flame with whom I was already working together for humanity for eons, in Egypt and in Atlantis.

I came here to this planet earth with an appropriate physical body for living in this 3-D (third dimension) reality. I was born in a certain moment with the astrological chart that I chose and was guided to have for this mission.

I was born on a small French island in the South Pacific. My parents were of the French noblesse. I am a direct descendant of the French aristocracy. I was raised Catholic. My father was a wealthy industrialist. It is on the family land that I grew up with my sisters. The family land covered the two most prestigious beaches where I was born that our grandfather, Roger, had the genius idea to buy shortly after World War II. This has created a lot of jealously to a point, and when my father passed away, people with influential position used their power to bypass the law to get to our estate. A mutual effort of the cabal, an archon infiltrated the family and a Jesuit/Freemason politician.

So I have been prepared by daily training sessions during sixteen consecutive months, which has tendered to keep me isolated from the world at large. My normal routine and my normal life were being set aside for preparation as I have been chosen to be the door to the Divine and for the preparation of the ascension and the shift of the energy.

During all these months, I was waking up in the morning and sat in the same corner seat the entire day, and the weirder thing is that my family has no recollection of it. It was like they were not able to acknowledge what was happening to me and until that day.

Then due to the mission I came to accomplish for humanity with my gifts in preparation of the ascension and beyond, I was con-fronted by many different dark energies—some were reptilians. And also I had to battle some dark mentalists, Archons. This has led me to many troubles as Archons can be invisible to the human eyes. They would broadcast information stolen, from one to another, to manipulate and twist the reality, troubles that I had not expected to encounter. But a curse had been placed on us, and I had to deal with these troubles. For three years, it was like a ride on an inferno roller coaster.

Before that, I met different people and I traveled a lot. I had life moments like everyone—some good and some bad—but thanks to all of it, I am here now in this exact moment of personal planetary evolution.

When I was six, I was playing on our swings under the banyans with my older sister. As we were playing, I ran in front of my sister, and her feet kicked on the side of my head. I was unconscious for a month. I had several near-death experiences.

I began to travel after that time with my father. I would go with him on his business trips, and we would talk about his experiences and my view of the world.

At twenty, I worked for a French airline. I would fly to Singapore at least once a month. I then would stay for five days all-expenses paid in a hotel, waiting for the plane coming from Paris to rotate back to the island. Other trips included Sydney, Tahiti, New Zealand, Jakarta, Vanuatu, Wallis, and Norfolk. During my layovers, I would visit local religious sites and speak to the people to learn about their culture and their beliefs.

I left the South Pacific and lived for five years in a Central American country that some refer to as the Latin American Swiss. Those five years had a big effect for me, in both good and bad ways. I discovered the real rainforest with its wild animals, scorpions, dangerous snakes, and dangerous waters. I was not prepared for those things. During that time, I had a terrible accident; luckily I was in a Land Cruiser. I have also met many different interesting people and situations—strange people. I also met many interesting people and made several good friends.

It is during our stay in Central America that my cousin Louis was diagnosed with cancer. This is how I began to become interested in natural food, natural treatment, and everything related to holistic healing.

I also heard of the clinic when I traveled with my cousin Louis to a natural clinic in Germany. My cousin's cancer went into remis-sion after using the combination of alternative medicine, prayers, and time with a Master in Tibet. In Tibet was where my cousin and I spent a week with the Master in the mountains of Kham studying. On our last day of meditation and learning, the Master gave me an emblem of a double Vajra from the neighboring country of Bhutan. The meaning of Vajra he told me was "the hand of the mighty me." It represents a bolt of lightning. This particular Vajra has been in the monastery's possession for hundreds of years, dating back to Alexander the Great. All the Masters that had known it were instructed to give it to the foreigner that had a gentle and life-giving heart. I was amazed when he told me it was mine to wear and to share its power with all others. I began wearing it around my neck from that day forward. The Master told me of its mystical powers and to use that power wisely. This alternative thinking and training prepared me to look beyond the veil of what I could see with my eyes. I could now see with my mind and heart. All of my experiences prepared me for what was to come.

In the early 2000s, I moved to the United States.

After extraordinary paranormal experiences of synchronic, coincidental series of events, my life had completely changed. Since these synchronizations that had happened to me, it brought to me people, books, events that have given me a lot of information on the manipulation of the weather, the disease sprayed, the prescription drugs, the calcification of the pineal gland by the fluoride, that every child at birth to be chipped, and the recollection of awareness of an ancient world behind. Not just the reptilian but more human forces are behind this attempt to knock down the world. And the recollection of who I am.

I was taken one day by surprise and touched by bad energy that hit me, but Jesus sent me help even before I realized what had happened to me. Then I had been confronted a few days later with a reptilian that offered me freedom.

Then I went to many other forms of trouble before I realized that I was battling an Archon that was controlling my blue flame, by manipulating its psyche since his very young age, and that did not want me to help him get his freedom.

I understood it when suddenly, without any reason, he said out loud while grabbing nervously the phone next to him in a sort of trance, "I got to call her. I have to call her right now. She is calling me. Katherine is calling me." This is how the Catharis, from the south of France, were destroyed by Rome, by Archons, and their knowledge was destroyed with it. Archons are manipulative forces outside human form and are the devil's forces, negative forces.

They are a parasite of human society; in many, many different forms, they access human psyche and manipulate our reality. They cannot create their own reality, but they take what exists and twist it. They lack the ability to express the creative force. But they are experts on taking what exists and twisting it.

They are energetic beings called Jen by the Islamic. Archons are the same thing; they manipulate and direct it the way they sustain parasite of human creativity, effort, media, and labor of energy.

Archons serve the reptilians and have created a network of bloodline families way back to represent their interest in invisible light and seat in top key places: media, ownership, school, churches, banking systems, government, and top intelligent networks. They are cold like the reptilians and show no sympathy. And these manipulative frequency entities are bringing their reptilian forces in human society, bringing their archonic world in our world more and more.

We have been manipulated for many years with interbreeding and genetic manipulation of human form. Before they hijacked our reality, humans were so different—they were living and creating from their heart.

We are holographic bodies of light with vortex called chakras, wheels of light, and that are the seven basic foundations, the one key to coherence of the heart. The heart, when in harmony, takes to consciousness. What they have done is to pull humanity into low vibrational, brain-dominated perception.

They have moved the point where the reality from the heart to the emotional chakra, to the seat of the emotions. And once you have done that, you have knocked everything out.

The belly is the emotional chakra, and through the atrocities done to us right now, we are going through many traumas—we do not operate from the heart. But the heart is the key, and it connects us very far up and in a far more expanded level of our awareness.

The Beginning of
the Tainted Angel's
Mystical Journey

My name is CHADD, though you can't spell my second name without Christ. I like to say, here I am on my sixth year, and I am attending the first school day of the year. I am already bored. After a few days, I think to myself, what am I doing here? What I am hearing is not interesting at all. I thought it would be fun to play with my new friends, but it has not been fun. I am here and bored! I began to attract the attention of the other children because I wanted to play. Hey, I want to have fun. Aren't we here to have fun? I do not understand why we have to stay quiet and still. It is simply boring and a waste of time. I already know what the teacher is saying. It is the end of the day, and I am now back home with no one my age to play with.

A few weeks after the school year began, my stepmother, Katherine, explained to me that my teacher Terry spoke to her and recommended I see a psychiatrist. The teacher was concerned that I may have attention deficit disorder and that I am possibly bipolar.

After a few days, we made an appointment to meet with the psychiatrist. My father and Katherine told me that the doctor knew what he was doing and that he would know what to prescribe me.

They said these pills would help me to concentrate in school and not disturb the teacher or the rest of the class. "Trust us," Katherine said, and I did. My long agony was beginning. So we went and I was prescribed my first pills.

I took them and at first it made me feel weird. My mouth was always dry, my lips too, and my stomach was upset. I was not able to move as quickly as I had before, and I also felt that I was not fully awake. When someone spoke to me, it was like I was in a dream state. My family said that it was normal, and if it continued, they would let the doctor know and that we would talk about it on our next visit. Every visit, we would inform the doctor about all the nasty side effects, and the doctor would say, "Let us try this other one," or "There is a new medication on the market that may be more effective." Then he would prescribe pills to address the side effects.

As years passed, I made little progress. The doctor suggested to my parents that it would be more beneficial if I entered a very specialized place where they could evaluate and monitor me for a seventy-two-hour period of time. He said they have access to the best available medications to effectively treat my ADD. Three to four times a year, an evaluation would be done, assessing how effective the treatment plan was and if I had made any progress. How well I was doing would dictate if I would be sent to the next facility. It went on and on.

Years have passed and now I am a grown man, but my routine is still the same. I go from facility to facility, sometimes for days, sometimes for weeks, and even months. I have been tortured and forced into overdoses time after time. I felt like a guinea pig. Several times I was stripped and placed onto a table and shot up with drugs against my will. One time the doctor refused to admit me into the hospital regardless of my injuries. He would convince my stepmother that it was not necessary. In the next facility I resided at, I asked the doctor if he could at least reduce the dosage and he did the opposite. He doubled it. Another time I was hospitalized in a psychiatric hospital or evaluation center for mental illnesses. I met an honest and responsible MD for the first time. He told my stepmother, Katherine, if she did not stop medicating me, I would simply die from it. Katherine disregarded the advice; she did not want to let go and listen. I was labeled mentally ill.

In my early years, we moved a lot because my father's job required it. We moved to a foreign country. As a child, my hair was very blond and the Middle Eastern people would pass by us in the street. They would fall to their knees when they saw me as if they had seen some kind of religious person. I also remember very well when my family would make me turn my head from time to time or put their hands over my eyes to avoid me seeing the public executions or beatings. I still managed to see and that will never fade away from my memory. I finally graduated, one year earlier than my classmates. I would go to the State Tech University where I obtained multiple degrees in various fields.

I finally reached my limit. I could not take it anymore. My mind was constantly in a foggy state. Taking all of these drugs affected my ability to think and function normally. I was depressed, ingesting pill after pill, going from one psychiatric hospital to another. To my dismay, I was addressed and treated as a retarded person. My rights were taken away from me. I could not continue to live that way. This was way too much, and I decided to leave that ugly world. I did not want to continue to take pills or be hospitalized any longer. I wanted a normal life. Luckily, I was able to realize that nothing was wrong with me, but I had to act too. It is essential that I take action or I would not survive. At that time, I had no one who understood me, no one to help me, and nowhere to go. There was no escape. I was trapped in the system. I decided to leave the unloving world.

I have escaped three near-death experiences. During my first experience, I saw vivid colors of the pastures and the crystalline waters. I heard beautiful music. During my second coma experience, I saw endless food on an infinite table. Everything was perfect and beautiful. There was peace. The third time I received direct training from God. God told me that I had a specific mission for him: to save souls and that I was the chosen one. God told me that I had to be born first and then die. This would allow me to be reborn into my spiritual and original family and come back with my original new

DNA and a higher level. God told me to have faith and that all would be made clear as things evolved.

How to escape when my family is complying with the demands of the system, the doctors, the facilities? How to escape when I am forced to take all these pills every day, several times a day? These drugs are killing me and keeping me trapped. My parents contributed to my misery. My stepmother would force the pills in my mouth and wait there until she was sure I swallowed them.

I decided to leave this unloving world. Suddenly, I woke up one day after eight weeks in a coma. I was not able to speak. Not able to move my arms or legs, I was alarmed to say the least. I could not walk and all kinds of tubes were coming out of my stomach and everywhere else. My ankles were severed for no medical reason. I could hear but I could not talk.

Now I am nineteen years old, handicapped and in a wheelchair for no reason. I'm forced to take drugs against my will, and they make me very sick. Katherine, my stepmother, has become my legal guardian as my dad continues to be sent every now and then out of the country by the company he works for. I do not feel well and I do not see any way out. Currently, I live in my father's house with Katherine. They made it clear that I had to stay on medication.

Here I am in a wheelchair, unable to live alone because I do not have enough money to pay rent. I cannot keep a job, but I am still trying to get one. These narcotics scramble my head. I am not my normal self, taking every new drug that comes on the market. I'm a guinea pig for the pharmaceutical companies and I cannot function. Moreover, I am trapped in my parents' home with a few hundred dollars from my government check to "live." Part of my check goes to Edward and Katherine, to pay for my room. Not much is left after that. I have no credit established, no personal account, no access to my money, and no one to teach me how to write a check... I am nineteen years old. All I have is a life of seclusion, which I have been experiencing for the eighteen years. Studying the Bible, listening and studying music, and following God's instructions is how I have passed the time.

As I stated before, during my eight weeks in a coma, I went to meet God and I saw fields of beautiful and vivid colors, an endless table with infinite food along with streets paved of pure gold. When I came back, I was gifted with the knowledge of sound. I was sent back by God, and I am an energy retracting transducer (speaker of God). I am the sound and VIE is the light! He told me that we are the God Duo, warriors of God, working for the highest government of the universe. God told me in order to control me, I would be labeled as bipolar, having ADD, being suicidal, and suffering a brain injury. I would be sent to jail and other times admitted into a state psychiatric hospital.

It was explained to me in a vision, by the Holy Father, that I had to go and fight for the freedom of humanity and free them from the satanic energies, the Reptilians. I was told VIE will fight along my side and that she was the only one I could trust. VIE had been with me in many previous lifetimes and was trained and prepared to help me. God told me that VIE would clean my DNA, giving me access to my memories and the ancient knowledge that were the necessary tools to win. I saw different levels of the battles. I saw what the people of high authority in the world were doing to keep humanity in slavery through prescription drugs that was poisoning and killing their bodies. The financial system, the pesticides put in our food, television sending subliminal messages to control the souls of humanity. They want to keep us misinformed through the media and in fear through the wars for power. Lastly, they manipulate the weather and have citizens receive vaccinations and antibiotics. They are killing us along with the plants and animals. Moreover, they also intend to put us in concentration camps, and that is when I was shown that my stepmother, Katherine, was a dark mentalist energy, a bloodline of the reptilians and a tool in their hands to keep me captive. And how she will eventually get Alzheimer's and type 2 diabetes.

They wanted my power and to control me. Katherine, being a dark force, knew me very well but had much difficulty manipulating me. She was cold and without sympathy, but she knew which buttons to push and would make me tell her everything about VIE and the work we are doing together. She would twist around all of the information to family, friends, and relatives in an attempt to destroy our work and reputations, all to create obstacles for us. Katherine cooperated with the powers that be as they kept me captive with barely enough food and water to survive. They wanted me to fear for my life as I became property of the state, being sent to jail, and, with a multitude of different mental health facilities, being forced to ingest dangerous drugs. As a result of taking these drugs, I have lost my sight. I saw Katherine in the courtroom and what she did through her eyes. She rolled her archon eyes, looking at them one by one, then entered their energy field. The judge and the lawyers were hypnotized, and their decisions were influenced to make sure I would be court ordered to go into in a mental health facility in a prison. I had envisioned the social workers documenting inaccurate reports regarding my behavior two months before I would appear in court. On a Tuesday review by the social workers, I was told that when I was released, I would have to live in a group home with two other patients. The system would be able to monitor me and make sure I stayed on drugs and in their control. I saw that I would be forced to ingest dangerous drugs beginning with the letter *R*. These two drugs with their horrible side effects, one being the development of agranulocytosis and severe neutropenia, were terrible. Both are dangerous due to the fact that they decreased my white blood cell count, which made me extremely vulnerable to infection and gave me suicidal thoughts. The second drug changes the chemical balance of the brain and can cause a heart attack, heart failure, sudden death, or pneumonia.

I was shown all the richest and powerful people in key places and how they try to destroy VIE and my work. I saw courts, judges, lawyers, and religious personalities, along with their churches, police-men, sheriffs, and politicians. They control the population through false or withheld information. All of these obstacles would be put in place to prevent the knowledge that we share and our metaphysical work for the good of the planet. Their agenda has allowed them to reduce the population and manipulate humanity, keeping us under their control.

Everywhere we went, new surveillance cameras would be installed. This would include our office, our homes, the bistro we ate at, shopping centers, restaurants, etc. Our institute would be vandalized, and sheriffs, police, and private investigators would constantly follow us. Our office building suddenly became government owned. I saw everything happen before it happened. These visions have been bestowed upon me because VIE and I are God warriors and God will not be defeated. The system will fall down, and their agenda will not come to fruition. Humanity will be free very soon. VIE and I are victorious in Christ.

The Policeman with a Nike Tattoo

VIE left alone to cool off on her side. She decided to apply some Light on herself and to listen to some biosound. Then she laid down, and VIE left her body for another journey on the other side.

She saw that CHADD called some people he met at the convention and told them that he was staying at a hotel on the beach. VIE had told him that she would meet him the next afternoon. Katherine was giving him some space.

VIE's first impression was not good, and she was right.

He was awakened by a loud siren that went off, and the lights turned on. She could see and hear CHADD. She was with him, but he could not see her from where she was. CHADD knew it was the fire alarm in the building but decided to ignore it, and instead he took a shower.

Then VIE saw herself arriving at the hotel, and she saw CHADD's car there, but he was nowhere to be found. She asked the doorman if he had seen someone in a wheelchair but was told a young man had gotten into a taxi. She was in shock; she didn't know where he went. She rapidly called the police in fear he had been taken against his will. When she went to the police department to find a detective to give him information, the detective told her that he had heard about a guy in a wheelchair that was taken to a hospital. VIE then drove to the hospital but was not allowed to see him. Now VIE is told by someone that she does not know that CHADD was kid-napped. He asked for his car to be brought to the valet area, and he was sent to wait outside the hotel when a taxi drove up to him and the valet forced him to get inside the taxi. CHADD felt he was kid-napped. After an hour drive, the driver pulled over to where a police car was parked. The driver casually got out of the car and so did the policeman.

At that point of the story, VIE was able to see that the policeman had a Nike tattoo on his foot and that a woman named Letica asked him to sign some papers, a bunch of papers. She gave him some keys to a beach house and offered him a job as a lifeguard and told him that now he was engaged to her daughter. And that this was all because of her.

Katherine drove them back home!

VIE and CHADD met three days later, and VIE asked him, "Do you understand what is going on? This woman is trying to buy you, or someone else is trying to buy you. Don't you see, what better way for the people that are out to destroy you than to make friends with you? She is offering you to be a lifeguard and you are handi-capped in a wheelchair! It does not make much sense."

Then CHADD suddenly realized and said, "No one will buy me. I am a man of God."

Then he erased her number from his phone and stopped answering her calls. Letica still harassed him with phone calls days after he erased the number, but he did not want to have anything to do with her.

The Big Saga Began

Three years of working and fighting Satan. It's been a little over three years today that we are battling against the curse that has been placed on us and the obstacles of dark forces. VIE's friend, Ron, the astrologist, told her one day, looking at her, "You are going to meet someone with extraordinary abilities." She did not know where. Only that it would be sometime in May.

But how can we explain to unprepared persons the meeting and reunion of two angels on earth with one common mission?

How can we explain that we are the God Duo working on "9.1.1. Mission Project" for the highest government of the universe? We can't! We tried though. How could we be taken seriously after the reputation and image that has been created by Katherine, my stepmother, of me all these years? She has ruined my credibility and my image. And all the trouble I have created unwillingly for VIE and I? My stepmother, Katherine, the Archon, has also a big part of it.

On my side of the family when I announced to them that I met VIE and was willing to work with her, their reaction was mutual; they would stand by Katherine's opinion. And my stepmom would find plenty of not very nice words toward VIE. Like that she was taking advantage of me, that she would use me for my money, that by the way I did not have, etc. She was the one taking care of my money and there was never any. We knew we had a mission from God together.

I was adjusting to living in the "real" world every day, like it is said. I would rather stay in this planet earth and with its inhabitants. We, VIE and I, knew that we had a common mission from God together. We decided at that point to work together. We got together again after ten days, and VIE began to work in the office with light and Sacred Geometric symbols, essential oils, and sound frequency to help my physical, etheric, and spiritual bodies. We met several times a week for a month, and I told her that I was feeling so much better now.

I was finally slowly beginning to adjust and balance in the third dimensional level and its gravity. After a month spending time with VIE and talking about the metaphysical world and what God was telling me, I went home and told my stepmother that I wanted to have surgery. A couple of days later, she told me that she had made an appointment in Tampa to see a surgeon to do the surgery.

We drove to Tampa and had lunch. Then we went to the hospital supposedly to meet the surgeon. When we arrived at the hospital, Katherine helped me into the wheelchair and pushed me into the hospital where two orderlies were waiting. She gave me to them. One the nurses walked over to me and took me into her arms. She was a big woman and well-endowed and pushed her face into my chest and said, "Smile!" I saw a flash and realized someone had taken a picture of me with this nurse.

Then I was moved to a private room. About an hour later, the doctor came into the room. I began to talk about surgery, but the doctor began speaking out my behavior. Then he told me that I was staying there for observation and treatment. They held me in place and injected me. I was screaming for help, but no one was there to help. I then was moved somewhere else and sedated.

They tied me to my bed naked again. I was afraid for my life. That was another nightmare. During that stay, anyone calling my home and asking to talk to me would receive the same answer from Katherine. "I am sorry, he had to be admitted again. He is so sick and nobody can visit him. I do not have any news neither. There is no communication or phone calls possible and no visitation admitted." Which was a big lie, as she came to visit me. She probably needed to feed herself on my emotions. And on VIE's side with her family, it was not much better the minute my stepmother decided that for once and for all, she would cut our mutual work. That she would cut and stop forever our friendship, and we would have to stop seeing each other.

She decided that she would separate the God Duo no matter what. With one exception maybe if there was some kind of money coming from our common work. Greed!

Her first action after the weekend out of town, she took my car keys, lied to me, and told me that we were going to have a cheesecake. Instead I was brought and admitted to a psychiatric hospital for evaluation. What does it have to do with me working with my gift received from God? I did not get it…

Then she contacted VIE's family. She took all that I had shared naively with her every night of our work during the days and twisted all the story against VIE. She went on to report that twisted story to her family that she met without telling me and my consent. She went into my personal belongings, found VIE's family contact, and Katherine began her sabotage. She made sure to let them know that she was a nice stepmom with a handicapped and mentally ill stepson in a wheelchair that she cared so very much for. She began corresponding back and forth, destroying me and my reputation and destroying the work VIE and I were doing, manipulating VIE's entire family to a point where it began to be practically impossible to work together, meet, or talk. She would do the same with my friends, and she made sure to have them on her side.

Little by little, when I began to get more and more out of the house and out of my seclusion, I realized all the damages she had done to my life. I began to clearly see that she has destroyed my life. I began to realize that it has also damaged my image. Family, friends, relatives, and neighbors were treating me without any respect or consideration, and I was having a very low self-esteem and a poor image of myself.

I was poorly clothed and I had no money, but I regained myself and made my way slowly with VIE's help.

VIE has always known who I was, and she has always respected me. She has always protected me and made sure that people were treating me respectfully. But the minute I would go back home, I was reduced to nothing. It took me a couple of years before I could openly talk about things that I had grown up with and that I had come to think that they were normal. And they were not. Like I never had any towels when I would take my shower and had to dry myself with my dirty clothes or sit at home naked on my wheelchair until I was dry.

Nothing that was mine has ever stayed very long in my possession. Relatives, family, or their friends coming in the house would go through my personal belongings and served themselves of my CDs, shirts, sunglasses...you name it. And this is the story of my life. A handicapped man, labeled mentally ill of ADD or bipolar, and who knows what else that Katherine likes to tell about me to the doctors, the sheriffs, my appointed lawyers, and psychotherapist, to the court I presume, police, friends, neighbors, family, and acquaintances since I was a kid. But what she did not tell is that I found out that some of my prescribed pills were not disappearing mysteriously because she was swallowing them.

Katherine was herself seeing a psychiatric doctor. She has been diagnosed with chronic depression. And lately losing her memory to Alzheimer's, but the pills were never strong enough for her, so she would take some of my prescriptions.

One day I was awakening in a mental hospital from an injection and found myself tightened to the bed naked and an orderly outside the door. I was monitored every hour by a female nurse. Then I was visited by a doctor that asked me very weird questions about what I was hearing and seeing. After three days of forced injection with medications, they gave me an overdose of drugs with terrible side effects to such a point that I could not talk anymore, neither was I able to transfer myself from my wheelchair, and I fell down in the toilet.

When I came back to my senses, I was lying naked on the floor in a fetal position, my eyes had dark circles, and one camera was filming the scenario. I screamed for help for over twenty minutes, begging for some help before a big black guy came to put me back in my wheelchair.

My tongue was a few inches from urine on the floor. Four days later, I was finally released.

That happened when they had to pump my stomach and had me ingest full of charcoal because they had overmedicated me. I came back home and reached to the phone to call VIE. I wanted VIE to see what my life was. I had round black eyes. Did they try to kill me? I think so. Why was I left so long on the floor while I was screaming for help?

Except for VIE, the fact that I was horrified and scared for my life and well-being did not seem to preoccupy or worry anyone else, and it did not stop my family from putting me again and again in mental hospitals. And even Baker Acting (I am referring to the Baker Act) me with the sheriffs to put me on psychiatric drugs and into hospitals. Can I be taken seriously and have any credibility after all these years of psychiatric drugs?

I have been prescribed medications and admitted to all these different facilities. These hospitals were certainly not going to deny my admission as long as the insurance would pay. There is no way it will stop after I have been processed in the government disability database.

Thanks to my dearly controlling stepmother, again. She wanted so much my monthly government check that she was managing. I had no personal account and no access to my money and did not even know the amount the check was for every month. You under-stand now why I had to reach for help and why God reunited us on that dimensional level, VIE and I. I needed help to get out of this mess. I am left very frustrated and I have a lot of anger. My life changed by this meeting at the Bistro, but I am still not my own.

Though, I am a Messenger of GOD, being reborn with a different DNA, my task is not easy.

Memory Altered by Drugs

We were guided to speed inside NSA private property, and that time and day, all went very well; roads were cleared for us. Then came the orange tree green day work, and where angels in a beautiful small white church offered us some refreshments. At the end of that day we were Baker Acted, intoxicated in a well-known hotel, and sent to jail.

The same way that it happened to at least three other women we know in some restaurants. Which means that many more are also intoxicated and sent to jail these days. Someone else was walking on her way to the gymnasium, stopped by an older woman that kept her a few minutes with some weird and bizarre questions, then came an ambulance where she was pushed in and admitted in a hospital, drugged against her will, and she remembered very well having something inserted inside her stomach.

Then came the trip to the state capital in the middle of the night. God guided us to take this trip to the coast. Followed by the Christmas where we were baptized together, the phone call to Elizabeth and Sebastian and to channel 09, and the final cut three years later (back to the future) where us the God Duo are again sent to jail.

Here is what happened that day.

For a few days, I am totally drunk by the Holy Spirit, and that morning, I took the car keys and I told my angel Light that I was driving and that we were going to work on a metaphysical level for the universe. We had no idea where it would end up. We were guided by the Holy Spirit. Still guided by Him, I put the perfect sound, per-fect wavelength for what we had to accomplish.

The people passing by the vehicle were reacting very well to that frequency. They were waving at the car or singing along with the music. They were happy with big smiles on their faces. We were doing what we were supposed to do, guided by the supreme force of the universe.

Now, understand that when you decide to come to earth you... um...you have no idea that you will forget it all, what you have planned for yourself and how you will live your life. So I was follow-ing the guidance I was receiving.

And...oh! It is so confusing now...my memory is altered. What is happening to me...oh! It is the mme...med...de...cine...to...to... the druuugs! They are poisoning me! What are you doing to me... who...where is VIE? Help! VIE, help me! RUBY? RUBY or VIE?

Ho! Ho! Is this the story or the other one? I am not sure. What are they doing...doing...with me.

Names have changed! Which are the real ones? Hum! But the main story...remains.

Ho, I got it! I understand now. They try to make...to kill me, they try to erase my memory. They are altering my DNA! Hum! It's okay.

The main story remains the same anyway. And no one can erase God or the Holy Spirit memory. Hum! Yes, of course, because it is already prophesied and no one can change it. God is in control. He has always been and He will always remain.

Ha! Ha! Ha!

He was, He is, He will always be.

So make your own opinion. It does not matter; anyway the result is the same.

God is the winner and so are we.

But you still have to make the right choice. So please read care-fully and follow your heart.

Yes, your heart because you have been disconnected and have become slaves, and you are supposed to act only through your heart. This is the big secret you have been looking for so long. *Love.* Yes! Love. Not through emotions.

VIE Sees Her Light Working Erratically, Glances in the Mirror, and She Remembers Katherine, the Dark Energy

I had gone back at my parents' house, and I could not reach VIE for days. Even my phone was not in my possession anymore, and I would have to ask for it when I needed to place a phone call, and someone from the house would listen to make sure I was in communication with VIE.

Then one day, I could not keep it. I called her and she picked up the phone. I wanted to meet with her; we needed to talk. I told her to meet me at the shop. When she saw me, she had a shock and I could see it on her face. After this last stay at the hospital, I knew that I looked horrible, I had lost weight, I was looking anemic again, and my skin was gray. I was perspiring by medication. I was feeling hot and cold, and my mouth was all the time dry, my lips were cracked. I did not know how to interact with anyone or sustain eye contact. I would always wear dark glasses. My eyes could not support the light, and I could hardly see her. I knew that I was horribly dressed, but she said that she could still see that I had a certain class and intelligence underneath my distressing appearance.

I have been labeled with various diagnoses over the years for ADD, brain damage, borderline personality disorder, and bipolar. Most of the drugs were addictive and had their own side effects. I had just started to show epileptic symptoms and an irregular heartbeat. A week after leaving the hospital, I began to show signs of bleeding ulcer. I was now unable to live and function normally. That is when over the following month I asked the doctor to lower the dosage of what I was on and the MD doubled the dosage instead. After a month of seeing the deterioration of my health, VIE could not resist. She decided to have a meeting with my stepmother, Katherine. She picked up the phone and asked her to come for a color harmonic session. She was hoping that by experiencing the natural therapy, she would see that she was not a treat for me and that instead she could convince her that I could get a normal life and make a living with my gift and she would feel relief, but VIE told me the whole story later on when we could meet again and talk.

VIE was in the process of beginning the session, and she glanced into the mirror at her face. She saw her face as twisted and not what she saw when she looked at her directly. And that is when she knew that something was strange about her. Because the light was acting erratically when it would hit her body. Her eyes were rolling and of a different look and color. And since that time, she knew that VIE uncovered her and never hid her eyes since then. They keep rolling and no one can really see them stable.

It is with her eyes that she hypnotizes and manipulates every-one that she meets. She uses her possessed eyes and gets into the energy fields of everyone she encounters. So VIE realized that my stepmother was a dark mentalist energy.

Then VIE began to have flashes and visions of the past. Now she could remember; she was already in battle against her in her pre-vious life and that it was Katherine who killed her. But her guides were telling VIE to relax, that in this life, she had no more power over her.

They also told her that unfortunately it is the power she had on me since I was raised by her. That is how she could manipulate me. VIE told me that it had amplified after I had received my gift and after I came out of coma. That she is now able to tap into my energy and tap into my knowledge. That she was the curse placed between us on this dimension and our common mission. And little by little, we had seen it. Sometimes VIE could guide me on time, and some other times, it has gotten us into many troubles. We are affecting the Reptilian's agenda and they do not like it. And by being manipulated by Katherine and the drugs is affecting VIE. It is making our work harder to accomplish.

The Middle Eastern Man in a Suit with Dark Glasses

That day CHADD was very agitated, he told me over the phone that he was having a bad intuition. I went to meet him at the park. Suddenly came a man walking in the park—a Middle Eastern guy with dark glasses and in a suit. It was quite a surprise as we were in summer and that day was very hot and sunny. Then he came toward us and said, "I am going to lay down on the bench for a while."

Then he walked away toward the bench located not far from the lake and laid down on his back on the top of his suit. Suddenly CHADD opened the driver's seat door, and before I could even realize what was happening, I saw him put one foot out, then he disappeared out of my view. I rapidly jumped out and went around, and he was laying down on one side in great suffering. I tried to helped him up, but he was too heavy and every move was extremely painful. I called the Middle Eastern man for help. He was the only one beside us in the public park.

I saw him observing CHADD from where he was. Then very slowly, he finally got off the bench and, taking all his time, walked toward us. He approached us, looked at CHADD, turned toward me, and said, "Leave him." Then he walked away, leaving me alone in the park with CHADD on the ground suffering. I rapidly went around the car, picked up my phone, and called 911.

It took twenty minutes and three more phone calls for the ambulance to finally show up, followed by a sheriff's car five minutes later after. While they were helping CHADD into the ambulance, I rapidly closed the doors and windows of his car and told the ambulance that I would follow them to the hospital to help him with the registration as he was dyslexic and had also lost the ability to write. On the way to the hospital, I was very concerned as I could see in the back window the man in the back, bent most of the time over CHADD, and I had never seen an ambulance driving so slow. We finally arrived at the emergency room, and I was asked to go by the front and to sit and wait to be called. It took another thirty-five minutes and many times asking the nurse at the front before I was finally showed the way to the emergency room, where he was. As soon as I entered and took a look at him, I saw that they had injected him with a strong sedative. His eyes were all red, and he was barely able to talk. A nurse came in the room with a blanket to cover him. She turned toward me and said, "I know that he may still be in pain, but they have injected him with a very high dosage of morphine and can't have more or his heart would stop beating."

CHADD was still waiting to get an X-ray. The lady nurse left and a man now entered the room and told CHADD, "I know that you must be suffering, and I am going to give you a shot of mor-phine." To which I rapidly replied, "You are certainly not going to do that. The nurse that just left told me that he already had a very high dose of morphine administered in the ambulance and that he can't have any more or his heart will stop beating."

He was released eight hours later with a plaster around his wrist to which he was allergic and had to go back to have it removed. What was that maximum dosage of morphine for on his way to the hospital? Who was this Middle Eastern man with dark glasses, and what was he doing in the park just when CHADD fell? Why was the parking lot slippery?

Meeting with the Pharaoh 1

I met Pharaoh 1 for the first time when he approached me in a public place and asked me to translate one of his favorite songs that was not in his first language. Then he disappeared, and I did not see him for nearly one year.

The second time was when I was with CHADD, and we entered that day the same place to have a bite. I did not notice him. We were sitting at the table talking when I saw him approaching me very slowly, bent and looking at me in a weird way. He came looking at me like as if he was going to either kiss me, slam my face, or like if I was a species he has never seen before—very close to my face. He stared at me, silent, for a very long time.

All this was so unexpected and weird that it did not occur to me to greet him. Finally he began to talk and told me, still with a weird look on his face and in a very bizarre voice, "The sky has brighter color and is a rainbow, the grass is of a more vivid green and lakes are crystal clear. The valleys and pastures are of melody..."

Then he turned toward the table where he came from and went to take his computer. He came back and sat next to CHADD, ignoring me completely for lapse of time. His girlfriend entered the place. He went toward her, talked to her for a while, then told us, "Please keep an eye on my belongings, I'll be back." He came back an hour and a half later. We made a comment, and he replied, "Oh! I went shopping."

Then he began to address me again. It was about a pope. Then he asked us to follow him to a very special metaphysical place. We left the parking lot followed by a motorcycle all the way downtown. He delivered us, then his message, and we all left to return home.

The Vision

I was explained in a long vision that I had to go and fight for the freedom of humanity—to free them from the satanic energies, the Reptilians and their bloodlines, the archons, that some named Jens. That this was my job and that VIE was sent to me to help me and fight with me. I was told that she was the only one I could trust. VIE had been with me in many previous lives and was trained and prepared to help me.

God also told me that when VIE had cleaned my DNA, I would have my memory back and that I would have all the knowledge and the necessary tools to win. I saw all the different levels of the battles. I saw what the people of high authority in the world and what they were doing to keep human people in slavery through prescription drugs that were poisoning and killing the body, or on psychiatric drugs that would keep them foggy and unable to function in their daily lives. Through the financial system and also pesticide put on the food, by using TVs and subliminal messages to control the souls of humanity in keeping misinformed, through the media, through the wars for power, the manipulation of the weather, through chemtrails from airplanes in the sky. And also I was told to be careful as the government would try to have the entire citizenship receive vaccination shots of antibiotics and to try to kill everyone including animals and plants and how they will be put humans in concentration camps.

And that is when I was shown that my stepmother, Katherine, was a dark mentalist energy, a bloodline of the Reptilians and a tool into their hands to keep me captive. And how she will eventually got Alzheimer's and type 2 diabetes.

They wanted my power and my control. And Katherine as a dark force, and knowing me very well, did not have much difficulty to manipulate me. She was cold and without sympathy, but she knew which button to push and what would make me tell her everything about VIE and my work. And then she would twist around all the information to family, friends, and relatives to destroy our jobs, our reputation, and to put many obstacles. I also saw when VIE and I would be intoxicated and that it would be a government (reptilians) set up with a Chinese couple, but I did not know when. But I saw, clear and vivid, that Katherine would Baker Act me several times and even sell me to the government and that I would be kept captive with barely enough food and water to survive. That I will then fear for my life because I would have become body property of the US state and I will be sent to a jail mental health place, where I will be forced for nearly a year to take dangerous pills with dangerous health side effects and that I will begin to lose my sight again due to the drugs. I saw Katherine in the courtroom, and I saw what she did through her eyes. She rolled her archon eyes, looking at them one by one, then entered their energy field to the judge and the lawyer's eyes to hypnotize and influence their decision just to make sure that I would be court ordered to a jail mental health facility.

I also had the vision that the social workers would release me a nasty news, two months before I am supposed to return to court, that my future was already more or less set up before passing in front of the judge in court. On a Tuesday review by the social workers, I was told that when I will be released, I would have to live in a foster house with a few other patients so that the system will be able to continue to monitor me and make sure that we will stay on drugs and into their control. I saw that I will be forced to ingest dangerous drugs beginning with the same letter R. Two drugs with horrible side effects like one that developed agranulocytosis and severe neutropenia, both potentially dangerous that decrease white blood cell counts, which cause extreme vulnerability to infection and give suicidal thoughts (that I had at a time), and the second drug that would change the chemicals of my brain and could cause fatal heart attack, heart failure, sudden death, or pneumonia to others.

I was shown all the riches and powerful people in key places and how they would try to kill me and destroy VIE and also our work. I saw courts and judges and lawyers and religious personalities and churches and policemen and sheriffs and politicians, and lies and control of the population though false or withheld information. And also governmental conspiracies against both of us as a warning because of the knowledge that we share and our metaphysical work for the good of the planet that is an obstacle to their agenda. That is to reduce the population, continue to manipulate human beings, and keep their control.

I saw how rapidly everywhere we would go, new surveillance and cameras would be installed, in our office building, in front of our houses in the Bistro we met, and in shopping centers and restaurants. I saw how our office institute would be vandalized, and we were followed by sheriffs, police cars, and private investigators. I saw our office management building changed to a government owner. I have seen everything before it happened.

I have been given these visions because VIE and I are God warriors and God will not be defeated. I know that the system will fall down, their agenda will not be completed, and people will be free very soon.

And that VIE and I are victorious in Christ.

Satan Exists

Behind the veil, there is a cosmic battle going on. Please believe me when I say Satan exists. We are facing the end of a cos-mic cycle. Some refer to it as the end of the Mayan calendar.

God is calling every one of his children back. In our work also exists what are known as reptilians. They are not a fantasy. They are surely real! They have been described throughout history by many civiliza-tions. I personally have faced one while attending a Qigong seminar. I mentioned the reptilians to an acupuncturist that was seeing clients there. I recommended that he read the book of Enoch on the disap-pearance of the earth. While waiting in line to access the bathroom when suddenly I heard, "There you are." I turned around to see who had spoken. I saw a short woman. I was keeping an eye on her since the first day of the seminar. She had been exercising with an oxygen tank. I then replied, "Me?" I told her to give me five minutes to use the bathroom and I would see her in the main conference room.

I went to the Qigong room and right there I saw her, and she was waiting for me with a reptilian. The reptilian's eyes were exactly like a snake, cold and bloody looking. They made me think about death. Their iris is vertical and rectangular. I immediately understood that I had to keep my eyes looking straight in its eyes. It was waiting for me to show the slightest sign of fear and then it would attack. I asked them what they wanted. They replied, "Would you like to have freedom?" To which I replied, "Freedom? How can you grant me something that I already have?" They gave me an avatar business card. I quickly grabbed it and left. While looking back, I realized the reptilian was nowhere to be seen. I asked the short woman, "By the way, what do you have?" I heard this horrible metallic voice when she said, "Don't worry, I am metallic." This was before the movie *Avatar* came out.

Since that episode, I have found that the reptilians have entered into a contract with our government to exchange their advanced technology for a quota of human beings so they can do their own research on human DNA and other experiments. I began to wonder if the reptilians and our government were behind the thousands of missing people in our country every year.

Control Plot

Similarly, after I received that information from the *Source*, I had been asked to share it with you. Archons, also known as Jens, are puppets of the dark forces who are here to distract and warp the truth. They are misinforming entities, and when one is seeking out the Jen for attachment, they are asking the Jen archon for infor-mation and answers. When a Jen is attached to a human being or is around, it is monitoring everything that is said, all the informa-tion they are hearing, receiving, or information that come out of the mouth. It has the ability to be like a broadcast tower or a radar tower when it is attached to someone. As soon as a person starts talking, the Jen has already alerted all the dark forces, and so the information that is coming out of that person's mouth is received by all dark forces and reptilians. This is an example of how the Jen acts like a broadcast tower center, saying, "Listen, everyone, listen, all of you now, listen carefully." Then they start changing the energy and affecting worldly people.

They start worldly situations, and they affect things, caus-ing them to change. The archon acts also like a policeman to be attached to someone. Then they report to everyone else what is neg-ative because they twist and deform reality. They get information to the dark forces, and then the reptilians can be warped. The Jens are working with fallen angels; they are working on a satanic level because their energy is to destroy light in the world to create dark-ness. This energy is to warp human beings so there is no salvation for them, so that humans can't be saved, and so that they fall further and further into darkness and under their control. This is a control plot that has been going on for a long time. They have been working through the politicians of various countries.

Additives such as chloride and fluoride have been put in our water, preservatives have been put in our foods, and chemicals are sprayed on our vegetables. Companies genetically modify fruits and vegetables in an attempt to control the masses like puppets. Airplanes leave chemical trails in the sky, which are very toxic and cause asthma, allergies, skin rashes, etc.

There is a war going on that has been deliberately kept hidden from the vast majority of people worldwide. This war is between the light and dark forces. These dark forces attack and deceive human-ity, and some are Jen entities that target spiritual individuals attach-ing themselves to them if possible (like Katherine has done with CHADD—being in a foggy state of mind under the influence of drugs, he became an easy prey for her to attach to). It was easy for her to manipulate CHADD. Katherine was able to put CHADD and VIE in incomprehensible situations and events for their surroundings.

They find out where you are vulnerable. It could be fear of los-ing money, sickness, mental health issues, or depression. They use your weakness, your fear, and negative energy to manipulate you. The dark forces warp the energies of the world around them and the people to make those greatest negativities come into reality. They have also infiltrated institutions that have done good things for the world (e.g., churches and the priests).

Katherine manipulated the surroundings, events, businesses, relatives, friends, and clients associated with CHADD and VIE. Once VIE received the news from the Higher Source, help and pro-tection was given to her and CHADD. Katherine's health began to deteriorate very quickly as her legs began to swell and her diabetes became serious. Unfortunately, Edward's health began to deteriorate as well.

The Meeting with Vie

For thirty-five years, I have waited for her. This was before, until the day I was guided to go to this place and look for...with copper. I did not know anymore, after these long years of seclusion, how to communicate with human beings. It took me one month of sitting in front of that public place trying to figure out how to find the courage to enter the Java Bean Bistro. I remember not having enough money, at that time, to pay for a cup of coffee until that day when I met her again. Her name was VIE, the one I like to call my angel on earth. We have met a long time ago, we have battled many battles, and we are reunited on this planet for the final one. And we already know that we are victorious in Christ.

A curse has been placed on us, and you will see what we have to battle and endure: we were asked to leave the place of our first convention, then Baker Acted, intoxicated, sent to jail, our office vandalized, and our furniture disappeared only to reappear—and we have to fight against Katherine's control and her dark work.

I found VIE on a Friday, and I was so excited I could not refrain from going home and telling my family. Katherine could not control her emotions and she reacted immediately. She could feel that something big was entering my life. And she had no intention to let me fly away free. She had no intention of letting me loose and letting go of her control. I was her toy to play with. I was like a butterfly caught in her net.

First, VIE had to get me back to health. She had to take care of me for four months before we could even think of working and battling together. Because when I found her, I was so sick, I could not think straight, I was blind due to so many years of so many different medications, which I had been taking for thirty years now. A drawer of each one pill that I have carefully kept in a safe place is not enough to contain it all!

I was asking VIE every day, "At what time are we going to eat?" I was so angry. And my hands were trembling so much that she would have to help me eat. It was already seven months that I had stopped all my medications, and my appetite was slowly coming back with VIE taking good care of me, nourishing me with the right food. Giving me plenty of Light sessions and vitamins and a lot of water, essential oils, and assessing my health progress with the office hand cradle. Little by little, I was coming back to life. I was sleeping less and recovering from blindness mainly due to the drug Risperdal. I was not incontinent anymore. My skin was looking better and better every day. I was still suffering from a bleeding ulcer, but my hands were not shaking as much anymore.

I decided to stop taking my pills even though my doctors stated that I could never get off the pills or I would die from withdrawal. I could not take their side effects anymore. Withdrawal was not easy; it was horrible, but I made it and felt so much better until the state authorities and my family decided that it should be another way.

I was now ordered by the government to be committed to a state psychiatric hospital (jail) and away from my hometown. The rehabilitation center where I was sent is not a handicapped accessible place, and there is no ramp, no bars in the shower, and no handle in the bathroom. I am very skinny and totally deprived of food and water. I barely had enough to survive. My wheelchair had been taken away and replaced by one very wide and heavy chair that does not fit through the heavy doors. My knuckles and fingers are bruised and wounded, and I have no Band-Aid that will fit or stay. The medications that I took for so many years altered my memory, and I have become insomniac. My sleep pattern has been altered also. The MD said that the lack of sleep is what had gotten me in so much trouble. I was sleepwalking awake during my days. My controlling Archon stepmother has hypnotized and convinced my psychologist and my lawyer that I needed medications. I was admitted into a state mental institution far from my hometown with no one to visit me.

I have a different way of thinking due to my DNA being altered by drugs, and they are going to continue to be altered to keep me in a foggy state. Once again, I am depending on some psychiatric doctors who have decided that my misbehavior can be treated by drugs.

I had told VIE that I would meet her again the following day, but Katherine had some other plan. She planned for us to go and visit a family member and to stay out of town all weekend. Yet VIE went back to the Bistro to meet me and waited for a few hours, but I did not show up. Luckily we were able to meet again the following week. I was looking for her and she was looking for me.

We were both at the Java Bean Bistro the same day at the same time. And this is how VIE still describes our first meeting. VIE was coming into the Bistro to enjoy a cup of coffee and read a book. Just in front of her was the table with Rocky, the motorcycle guy, she likes to name it this way, and me a handicapped man in a wheelchair who was wearing very dark glasses.

I was malnourished, obviously anorexic, blind, incontinent by the side effects of the drugs on my bladder, and unable to express myself correctly due to the effects of the drugs. My eyes could not support the light, and because of the medications I had taken, I was blind. I was poorly dressed, but she could see I had a certain class and a friendly personality. She was facing the entrance and exit door. She could not avoid being part of something that happened. A woman on her way out was evidently attracted to Rocky, and she was doing all that she could to make him see her. She stopped at our table, and VIE told me that she was shocked by the rude attitude and impolite behavior of the woman toward me. She acted as if I was not there. I simply did not exist in her eyes. And VIE continues, "I could also catch the sweet and loving energy coming from you." Then the woman left, the motorcycle man left, and I turned myself, but instead of facing her, I presented my right side to VIE as I was looking at the wall in search of some scriptures to read and to use to begin our conversation.

Then I began to talk, still not looking at her, and said to her, "What do you do?" That was what was written on the wall, and she replied, "Well, something that is very different. I am a Light worker. That is one that works the Light and Sound for living."

Then I replied to her, "It has been thirty-five years that I have been waiting for you. I am reconnected to my spiritual family as you are, and I am a speaker of God. I am an energy retracting transducer of God. We are both two missionaries on earth." Then I showed her the back of my wheelchair in which was written "Cross Fire" and the design of a blue flame. I moved from the wheel chair to the leather seat that was empty next to her and thus began a very long and interesting conversation.

We came to realize that we were already working to prepare ourselves to enlighten. She was amazed when I told her that I was drawn to this place because I felt a vibration coming from her. I could hardly see her. My sight was reduced and very blurry and I could barely see, but I managed to find the coffee shop as I was drawn to come and meet VIE again.

I could sense and feel her. My senses were very elevated. I told her, "I found my way to you by a phenomena that is remote viewing and echolocation." We exchanged names and started a very interesting discussion from which I got the confirmation to our extreme conviction that we were already working behind the veil for some time and that we have lived together in previous lives.

I asked VIE when we were alone about the Vajra and how it was creating such an amazing sense of well-being and energy. She told me the whole story behind it. She told me that this particular Vajra had been in the monastery's possession for hundreds of years. And that all the Masters that have known of it were instructed to give it to a lady named VIE who had a gentle and life-giving heart. The Master told her when he gave it to her of its mystical powers and to use that power wisely. It was created to be worn all the time because it helps to heal physically, emotionally, and transmits healing energy and blessing energy. The transmission of blessing helps to heal the etheric field, which is God. It is the pulse of the matrix that holds everything together.

This is why VIE and I have been Baker Acted, intoxicated against our will, arrested, and sent to jail for the first time. It was where and when VIE's Vajra was removed and disappeared and was not returned when we got out of jail the following day. We remem-bered very well that before we were intoxicated against our will, there was a mystical old Asian couple who looked very serious and out of place. When they arrived, they sat not far from us. Neither were talking or drinking, and they were just looking straight forward. And there was not much to look at. What were they doing? Is there any correlation with them and the disappearance of VIE's Vajra? Most probably! A Chinese old couple and a Vajra from Tibet! They knew the power of it.

On my side, I was asked to remove the ankh VIE had given me, instructing me to wear it and to never take it off, as it was my protection and linked to her to protect me. My ankh was removed from my possession and also not returned. Until that day when it mysteriously reappeared on my stepmother's neck. I asked her how she got it. She was unable to tell me. I asked her to give it back to me. When I put it back around my neck, it first made me feel like someone was watching me. A few days later, I found out that the ankh was possessed by an entity that was trying to enter my body. I was shaking and coughing and turned violet—I could not breathe. When VIE heard me suffocating, she jumped out of her seat and ran toward me. Took the ankh rapidly off my neck and reached to her light. She began to donate some light colors, and VIE was talking in the language of the light. I could see a few minutes later when I began to breathe again that it was a kind of red color and a Sacred Geometric symbol that she was using. I asked her about it, and it is when she told me how she was trained for before we met and how she also is totally guided by powerful other forces on the other side of the veil.

During that summer, everywhere and every time we would be together, we would be followed. In the Bistro where we were every day, we would see a man sitting with glasses and a computer.

He would listen to all our conversations and would be taping and recording them. After a while, another person would be doing the same task and would replace him. When we are seen together in public, there were always lights of flashes from pictures taken of us. When we were driving on the highway, we would have the military following us. Around town, it's either county, sheriffs, police, etc.

I Woke Up One Morning
and I Was Not Sure Which
Dimension I Was In

My life seemed so different, I was thinking, drinking my morning coffee. What happened to me? Where am I and where do I go? Where is my blue lagoon? What has happened to my life? What is next now?

That is when I saw in a local magazine a seminar featuring Dr. Pearl. I took the seminar and was lucky as it was given by Dr. Pearl. I attained my certification in reconnective healing, the reconnection trans-meditation. I remember quite well the story of a man that had a very advanced cancer and got healed. In my mind, during the session with Dr. Pearl, he had such a different energy and glow that no one questioned or had any doubt that it was true.

I was still looking for something else. Something was missing until I found the Light and Sound therapy and spectra harmonic and frequency healing. That day I knew this was it. That it was what I was searching for and that I did not need to search anymore. I flew to Canada and met someone that became my friend. She was kind enough over the phone to take the time to answer all of my ques-tions. That day I decided to go to take the first plane leaving in her direction to go and meet her. I remember being impressed by the quality of the people that were there for the same purpose.

Then I was guided to take a four-day workshop of supreme Qigong. It was taught by one that I would call a great teacher. It was an outstanding weekend.

There were over 2,500 people together at the seminar. Amber, whom I did not know, kept passing next to me and where I was seated. She seemed to be very nervous. I had the vision that she was very stressed out and lonely. I felt that she was quite depressed. I knew that I had to help her and do something very quickly before she would. Possibly she would threaten her own life. She was very agitated.

So we went in a small and private seating area not far from the bathroom, and I began to reconnect her to her angels. Luckily, because she did not know me, she confidently let me work and gently opened her heart to receive. Since then, Amber never forgot me.

She received that day the joy that the reconnection to the cre-ator brings. And the strong feeling of sudden peace from love and the bliss that comes with it when you are reconnected. Tears of joy were rolling down on her check, and she kept saying, "My God! I never experienced such a thing. Thank you so much." It feels so good.

Then one day, another amazing experience happened while I was in Vegas, where I was presenting and demonstrating the light on people. I suddenly felt a strong energy coming from the far end of the room to which I was very much attracted. In between short light sessions, I left to see what that strong energy was and where it could come from. I was guided to pass in front of a Tibetan shop; I passed it and was drawn to enter a conference room. Where to my amazement at the far back end was a huge pyramid with gigantic crystals poles and under it an empty seat waiting for me.

I went straight to it, sat, and entered into an altered state of awareness—to a point that I did not realize that somebody in the front of the conference room was giving a speech and he was under no light but in the dark. It was impossible to see who was giving the lecture, though there was someone on stage. After a certain time, I came back into my body and finally left still walking as if I was floating. I passed the entrance door to exit, and it is at that time that

I heard from two Tibetan nuns standing on each side of the door, saying, "It must be a very specific and precise time on the planet for Him to come out of his retreat from Shambhala and to speak in public in the United States." At that exact same time, I began to receive clear visions of Sacred Geometric symbols. Hurting the aura of the person, so intense. From that moment of reception and vision, anyone passing by me and that was close to my aura would feel my aura and I could detect the imbalance of their body. It was quite an amazing experience, but also it was very challenging. I had to learn to avoid being too close and to retract my own aura.

Following this event, I decided that it was time for me to pack my bag and go and visit this Tibetan master. I spent a week with the master in the mountains, meditating and praying. On my last day, the Tibetan master gave me an emblem of a double Vajra. The meaning of Vajra is "the hand of the mighty me" and represents a bolt of lightning. I was very moved and amazed when I realized that it was mine to wear. I began wearing it around my neck from that day forward.

After a couple of years, it had gotten so much that its power attracted me to trouble that I had not foreseen with the Chinese cou-ple, but one night I will be able to have all answers while I was back to my other life.

What Do You Do?

It was just another day in sunny Florida. I got dressed, put on my Vajra, and off I went to my office looking forward to an uplifting morning of meditation. I decided to stop at the coffee shop to enjoy a cup of coffee. While checking my messages, I had a sudden premonition. I felt today would be unlike any day I had known before. Immediately I was taken back to an astrological chart reading that had been done by my good friend RC. He foresaw me meeting a good person with extraordinary abilities. "Now is the time for the reunion of the angels with one common mission, to serve humanity." Those words would have a profound effect on me.

As I regained my senses, I noticed just in front of me was a table with Rocky, the motorcycle guy, and a handicapped man in a wheelchair who was wearing very dark glasses. He was blind, malnourished, and unable to express himself correctly. I felt an instant connection to this individual, whom I had never met before. He was horribly dressed, but you could tell he had a certain class and friendly personality. I was facing the entrance and exit door. I could not avoid being part of what would happen next. I noticed a woman who was clearly attracted to Rocky, doing all she could to make him aware of it. She stopped at their table. I was shocked by how rude and impolite she was toward the handicapped man, acting as if he did not exist. I could catch the sweet and loving energy of the man in the wheelchair whom I could only see the back. Then the woman left, and a few minutes later Rocky left. The handicapped man was the only one left.

He suddenly turned his wheelchair, but instead of facing me, he faced the wall on my right but was in front of me. I would then only see him from his right side. I had wondered what that was all about, and then he began to speak to me, still not looking toward me, and said, "What do you do?"

I thought this meant for living. He was reading the inscription on the wall, and that is when I replied, "Well, something very different. I am a chromotherapist. One that works with Light and Sound for healing."

He replied, "I am reconnected to my spiritual family as you are, and I am a speaker of God. I am an energy retracting transducer of God." We are both two missionaries on earth. Then he showed me the back of his wheelchair in which is written "Cross Fire" and the design of a blue flame. He moved from his wheelchair to the leather seat empty next to me, and we started a very interesting conversation.

We realized that we were already working to prepare ourselves to enlighten. To my amazement, he told me that he was drawn to the shop because he felt a vibration coming from me. He said, "I have been waiting for you for thirty-five years." He could not see and could hardly hear me. His sight was reduced and very blurry and he could barely see, but he managed to find his way to the coffee shop as he was drawn to come and meet me.

He could sense and feel me. His senses were elevated. He found his way to me by the phenomena known as remote viewing and echolocation.

We exchanged names and started a very interesting discussion from which I got the extreme conviction that we were already working together behind the veil for some time.

When CHADD and I were sitting at the table alone, he asked me about the Vajra and how it was creating such an amazing sense of well-being and energy. I explained to him that the Vajra is designed to be worn all the time, anywhere between the heart and the throat. That it had a bright ruby that was a symbol of royalty. The solar form has a double *dorje* Sacred Geometric design and transmits healing and blessing energy. It helps to heal physically, emotionally, and to develop and strengthen virtue and self-realize the divine nature. It has meditative effects that allow one to be more in the moment and to be able to respond to others in love, rather than react, helping to truly develop more harmlessness in all aspects of life. It attracts alignment of the soul with the personality, raising the lower centers of personality energies, up into the higher chakras, the heart, throat, brow, and crown center while the corresponding lower centers are purified and transformed for personality integration with the soul. All the head centers are stimulated as higher telepathy replaces lower psychic projection. The rainbow bridge of the Monad. Soul and personality can develop and transcend limiting forces and karma from past lives and this life.

The transmission of blessings helps to heal the etheric field. The etheric field is God. It is the pulse of the matrix that holds everything together. Through your humility, you ask God to work through you, not to be in charge of you but to cocreate with God. It is the intellect that causes separation, and it is through the etheric field where the past, present, and future, the mind, emotions, and the physical all come together and can be healed.

It is a double *dorje* Sacred Geometric design with four etheric weaver crystals aligned in perfect symmetry, together with a diameter blue Siberian quartz crystal and disc on the back that allows the form to resonate with the cosmic sacred geomancy of the individual. The crystal has an applied color therapy. The crystal disc is etched with the sacred geomancy of the Sri Yantra.

The form comes with precious stone set in the center. The wire used to wrap the crystals is copper and gold, which helps to increase and amplify the resonance of blessings transmitted through it.

I had told CHADD about myself, but I wanted to know more about his special abilities that drew him to me and how we were brought together.

He told me that he is often locked in the house and is kept medicated to sleep to almost noon. One morning, he woke around 8:00 a.m. because of a dog barking and sensed a powerful energy. He was able to use his special ability of remote viewing and could see through my eyes as I drove down Orange Avenue to the coffee shop. As he could see me driving, he quietly turned off the alarm, opened the door, and left the house without making a sound.

Once he got to the sidewalk, he needed to focus on the energy, remote viewing, and a special ability called echolocation. So he would click his tongue and evaluate the echo when the sound reflected back to him. Since he could hardly see and his third eye could only sense a few feet, he had developed this unique skill to navigate. This is a technique that bats use to fly in dark caves.

CHADD then began to tell me of the last seventeen years of his life. It all began when his father and stepmother had seen him as a threat and had his psychologist have him committed. This first step led him to being sent to the mental ward at the local psychiatric hospital.

He doesn't remember much, if anything, of what happened before he went in the hospital and when he was growing up. His mother told him that he was immediately drugged and put under the influence of mind-altering drugs to control him on that warm summer day. He soon fell into a coma. Coma is a divine thing; time is irrelevant during a coma. Christ was frozen inside of him, and heaven was very comfortable. It was all so beautiful, the sound and vision of heaven made him feel he never wanted to come back. He saw plush images, many animals and loved ones on the other side; he knew he had a mission in this life.

Before he fell into a coma, his eyesight was gone. When he moved into the coma, he was not deaf because God gave him an amazing ability to hear. He could hear every conversation that was held in the room and remembered them all. For seventeen years, he had used the gift of sound to listen, observe, and navigate his way in his surroundings.

He never displayed this ability to anyone but his mother and now me. All of his senses were elevated except for his sight that was severely influenced by the drugs that he had been prescribed. This gift of hearing had made him extremely clairsentient and psychic. During the last seventeen years, he had had three near-death experiences. The first was when he was committed when he was twenty. During that first experience, he said his training, his life, came directly from God. That God had a specific mission for him to save souls, but sometimes God has one follow unusual paths. He had to die three times for unknown and spiritual reasons. God told him he must have faith and that all would become clear to him as he evolved even further. God told him also that he had to be born first, then die, and to be reborn into his spiritual family and come back with new DNA and a higher level.

Through all of this, CHADD did not know why God had forsaken him. He felt like Job. He wanted to believe and have faith. I could see that his thinking was very cloudy because he was under the influence of the medication. His clarity of thought was altered by it.

I asked about his family. He told me he lived with his father, Edward, his stepmother, Katherine, and his half brother, Paul. His mother, Ethel, lived very close to the coffee shop. CHADD would visit her once a month and stay the weekend. He said she had emotional problems, and she had divorced his father when he was five. She had never remarried and had fought for his freedom since the time his parents split up.

I asked about his life before he was committed to the mental hospital. He told me he had no memory of that, and if I wanted to know more, I should ask his mother. So off to see his mother we went.

I was now prepared for my life-changing experiences and a world I had never known before. How was I to know that my world would all change because of a cup of coffee? I was entering a world of lies, deception, hope, and pain. My spiritual journey was about to begin.

Cutting the Angel's Wings

Driving with CHADD was very interesting; at times it seemed as though he was reading my mind, asking me about my psychic and metaphysical experiences. Especially considering how he learned to live with both of his Achilles tendons having been cut in the hospital to control him.

I asked him to tell me about his mother. I could tell I touched a nerve with that question. He told me that he doesn't remember much about his childhood with his mom, but when he was in a coma, he could hear her speaking to him, telling him that she loved him and would not leave him, that he was special and had always been. He didn't exactly know what she meant by that, but he knew she really loved him.

When he was conscious again, she would visit him every day in the hospital. When he was able to leave his room, she would put him in a wheelchair to take him for walks down the halls of the hospital. She told him they were never alone; there was always someone following them. He had lost his sight because of the drugs, so he never saw anyone.

CHADD said that she also had her own set of problems. She was very emotional and moody. When he would stay over at her house twice a month, he would hear the sounds coming from several pill bottles several times a day. He never knew why.

We finally arrived at the house. It was a small house with several oak trees in the front yard. The grass was green and had a brick entryway with double doors. It had a strange symbol hanging on the front of the house that you had to walk past to get to the front door. It had a strange familiarity to it. I could see by the bowl sitting near the front door that she owned a cat.

I helped CHADD out of the SUV and into his wheelchair. I pushed him up the little ramp toward the front door. He could sense where the doorbell was. He rang it, and a few moments later the door opened slightly, and I could see someone peering out at us.

"CHADD, who is that with you? Does your father or your stepmother know you are here?"

CHADD said no.

She replied, "Who is this woman, one of their friends?" CHADD immediately told his mom that he had met me by

chance at the coffee shop and he knew he was meant to meet me today. He also told her of his "great escape" from the house when everyone was sleeping.

It was still very early, and usually his father leaves for work at 7:00 a.m. and his stepmother sleeps in until 9:00 or 10:00 a.m. CHADD is always expected to sleep late, so he knew he had a limited time to see his mother. On this day, CHADD knew he had to leave right after his father slightly after dawn and navigate his way down the sidewalks to the coffee shop. It was obvious that he had special abilities—abilities I had never seen before.

His mother invited us in. After we entered, she looked outside to see if anyone had followed us. That behavior caught me by sur-prise. CHADD had told me she was a little eccentric, so I was some-what ready for it. We went inside and sat down on the couch. She turned on the lights and did not open the blinds.

CHADD's mother introduced herself as Ethel. I told her of how I met her son, and then we started to talk. I asked CHADD if I could ask a few questions of his mom, and he said, "Certainly." There were things he would like to know also even though he did have time over the years to ask questions, but sometimes his mind was stuck and he couldn't think properly.

Ethel was very hospitable and asked me if I wanted something to drink. We had just left the coffee shop, and I wasn't ready for anything else to drink. I knew time was of the essence, and I began to ask her what happened that caused CHADD to go into the mental institution.

What she was going to tell me was far beyond anything I had expected. She told me that CHADD's life started very unusually, but it would take a lot longer to tell. That it would be a story for another day. He had been in seclusion from the age of eighteen until thirty-five and had very little contact with the outside world.

She still did not trust me. She asked me to tell me more about myself and why I was interested in her son. I told her about my path to the light, what I had seen. When I told her everything, I thought she would think I was crazy. To the contrary, she told me she knew of things that most people would consider mentally unstable. And over the years since she and CHADD's father had divorced, she herself had spent several stints in mental institutions. Plus she was still taking many prescription drugs that she wishes she could stop taking, but she felt she couldn't live without them. I asked her what medications, and she told me. Adderall, Ativan, Prozac, Depakote, etc., drugs that are very addictive and could be more destructive than helpful. She considered the world of prescription drugs as a way of controlling people; this is a belief that we both shared. After that discussion, she was a little more at ease.

She began to tell me that CHADD's father had called her to let her know that CHADD had threatened him and his wife. CHADD was acting irrational and seemed to be under some illegal drugs, and CHADD was sent to the hospital. His father knew the police chief very well, being a government attorney and often worked with him on federal cases, so getting his way was very easy to do after CHADD came back from Punta Cayenna.

Ethel didn't believe him. She knew that he was always very secretive and that his entire life was in protecting the government no matter if it was right or not. To him, the government was always right. The government had something to do with the situation.

Edward informed the police that CHADD was violent and had a history of mental illness. At that point, the policeman, Baker, put him in handcuffs. CHADD couldn't call his mother because his father took control of the entire situation. He had CHADD's psy-chiatrist, Dr. Earl Waitt, meet his wife and him at the hospital. The doctor used to come for dinner when Ethel was married to Edward; she knew him well. The doctor and Edward would disappear into the study and wouldn't come out for hours while Ethel would make small talk with his wife. That is where Ethel first came to understand the effect of prescription drugs and how these drugs can be used to control people.

Ethel did not know what happened to CHADD for several days. Every time she would call CHADD, his cell phone went directly to voicemail. When she would call Edward, she was told CHADD had left the house and he didn't know where he was. Edward finally told her with his deceptive monologue.

By a strange coincidence, CHADD's only real friend, Madeleine, was a nurse at the hospital and worked in the same ward where CHADD was taken. She watched what was happening to CHADD when he was admitted for about a week. Madeleine had called Ethel when things seemed to be very wrong and things were not being done according to procedure. When CHADD arrived at the hospital, he was immediately strapped onto a dolly and rolled into a private room. He had a sedative administered within seconds of him entering the room. To Madeleine, it was so well coordinated that it seemed preplanned. She saw Edward, Katherine, Dr. Waitt, a resident doctor named Dr. Luke, and a soldier. The soldier's face was very stoic and also very unusual. He had a very thick and deformed forehead and seemed to be very fit. They were huddled closely in the waiting room down the hall from CHADD's room.

Madeleine saw all of them enter CHADD's room, and then she was called in. CHADD's father and stepmother didn't recognize her because she never went to the house where they lived. CHADD felt very uncomfortable having her come to the house and never men-tioned her name to anyone. Madeleine remembered that and didn't tell anyone that she knew CHADD.

Dr. Luke then instructed her to administer 100 ccs of Procolin. Madeleine immediately asked if she had heard him clearly. She did as instructed even though she knew that the dosage she was directed to give CHADD would immediately put him into coma. During the next week, she saw several other people go into the room, and there was a sentinel posted at the door. She had never seen anyone that was Baker Acted, have a guard posted at their door. Only military prisoners had been given such treatment.

Madeleine also saw unusual things happening to CHADD. A pint of blood was taken from CHADD twice a week. That was very unusual, and she began to wonder why. She knew that he was type O negative and could be used with any blood type, but the drawing of blood so frequently was against all existing guidelines. When she voiced concern to Dr. Waitt, she was immediately removed from caring for CHADD, but she still worked on his floor and could see the activity that was going on.

Over the first week, more strange-looking government employees clustered day and night in CHADD's room. Madeleine didn't see CHADD leave the hospital. He was moved when it wasn't her shift. She knew something was wrong. She feared for his life.

CHADD could hear the conversations from the first day in the hospital. His father, doctor, and the person who called himself Dru were all in the room shortly after he was sedated when admitted. Not only were they discussing what they were going to do with CHADD but they were also wondering who else had CHADD told about them.

They said that they had decided that once they moved him to a secluded government hospital, they would awaken him for interrogation. They were also interested to find CHADD's medallion that he was not wearing when he was picked up by the police. CHADD was initially taken to a section of the hospital that was mostly vacant. He could feel strange vibrations coming from this area. He could telepathically hear the thoughts of two other young men being held there. They were not as gifted as CHADD but different than most, and they were screaming out for help. CHADD had been stripped and placed onto a table. He was injected with several drugs against his will. On a table next to him was a mother to be that was begging for her baby's life and was screaming out, "Murderers!"

The orderly rolled CHADD into his room, leaving his arms and legs bound to the dolly. As he was lying there, he heard a famil-iar voice of his charge nurse, Madeleine. She told him she was there and would take care of him as much as she could. She walked out of CHADD's room and immensely concerned for CHADD when she saw his father, Dr. Waitt, and Dru.

During the week of CHADD's stay in the hospital, he knew they were taking all kinds of tests in his room. He was becoming a blood donor and being taken to different parts of the hospital for CAT scans and other tests he knew nothing about. He did not know why all of these things were happening to him but would find out later.

CHADD was now totally under the control of Edward. He had been given massive amounts of drugs and had his Achilles tendons cut, so he needed a wheelchair to get around.

I had taken up much of Ethel's day, and I could see she was get-ting tired. I thanked her and asked if she could arrange a meeting at the coffee shop with CHADD and her for the weekend coming up. She told me she would do her best.

With that, I thanked her for the information she had given me and left for the day, anticipating a meeting with CHADD again.

The Archeologist's Personal Journal: The Messiah Waneka, the Christ Wavoka, and the Antioch City

E thel gave me this book before I left, and she told me to read it carefully. Many of the answers to questions that I had would come to me through this book. She also told me to look for hidden meanings in things. She knew she was not strong enough for CHADD and others, but she believed I had the will and determination to help save the light.

Henri was a world famous archeologist who was the model for the movie character *Indiana Jones*. He kept explicit notes on his life and his work. For the most part, organization and documentation were the ways of his life. They were who he was.

In Henri's Own Words: My Great Adventure

I was born outside of Browning, Montana, on the Blackfoot Reservation on October 13, 1900. My parents had moved from Texas two years earlier and received approval from the Blackfoot tribe to build a ranch west of Browning and close to the Glacier National Park to help them develop their new source of survival cattle.

My father was an avid hunter and fisherman. He had traveled to Montana a few times to enjoy the outdoors. He was also a man of honor, and the tribal elders could sense that. My father would help them any time they needed him. He would help with building or farming projects or help as an interpreter when asked.

My mother was also trusted and a person that was in harmony with nature. She was sensitive to what was going on in my and my father's life and was always there for us. I didn't have any brothers or sisters.

I lived a childhood where I was surrounded by great natural beauty, a land of unpredictability. There were earthquakes, floods, and storms without warning. And at that time, there were many wild animals to contend with: bears, wolves, and mountain lions. I became a skilled outdoorsman from my father, Indian brothers, and the Blackfoot tribe members that treated me as one of their own.

White Eagle was the chief of the tribe; his medicine was the white goose. He would wear the head and tail of a goose on his head-dress decorated with two narrow pieces of red flannel, which steamed back over his shoulders. He was also an eagle shaman, and when not wearing his headdress, he wore a magnificent eagle feather entwined in his hair. He was well over six feet tall and was an imposing figure of an invincible warrior. White Eagle had many tragic moments that he had to navigate during his life. His tribe members depended on him; there was no other who had the skills to help everyone except for him.

I heard the stories of Ghost Ridge, Big Crown Rock, Two Medicine River, and the Ghost Dance and how the tribe believed that Christ came back as an Indian called Wavoka.

All of these things happened during a hostile time for the Blackfeet in Montana. In the late 1800s, many starved to death and supplies were rationed only once a week, and they were minimal at best.

I became close friends of White Eagle's son Willie Brightfeather. We would spend many hours listening to his father telling tales of mystics and spiritual events that were part of Indian lore.

I learned then that there was a remarkable difference between Western prophecies and those of native peoples. When Western prophets see into the future, they envision Armageddon, the end of the world. When native prophets look down the same path, they see the completion of a great cycle, a change of worlds.

The reason of these vastly different views is found in the way time is experienced. In the West, time is history, there is a past, a pres-ent, and a future—a beginning, a middle, and an end, like a stick. Native people experience time as a cycle. There are four stages, such as the seasons: spring, summer, autumn, and winter. Like a hoop, each stage is a preparation for the next. At the center of the hoop is a still timelessness, the eternal present around which the cycles revolve. The visions of native prophets occur at that center point from where the cycles of change can be seen. There is no end.

White Eagle told us about Drinks Water, a holy man of the Sioux. An ancestor of many moons ago, his vision occurred long before the coming of the whites. Drinks Water saw a change of worlds, and it was more than he could endure that he died from sorrow. White Eagle, in his wisdom, told his son and me that when interpreting dreams or prophecies, it should be remembered that a literal approach is often misleading. That is particularly the case with the prophecies of Drinks Water. Rather than the end of the world, what is implied is a transformation of consciousness from one view of the world to another and the emergence of the new world.

For years, the shamans had prophesied the end of the earth cycle, the disappearance of the white man, and the return of all living things that had vanished under the pressures of world. He told us the time was near; even his Indian brothers, the Mayans, had predictions of a new world order that existed for many seasons. He said only by honoring Mother Earth can we avert disaster.

He told us to always remember that the scientist and explorer in us functions out of the conscious mind, the prophet from the uncon-scious and our hearts. To not only use our minds but our hearts to guide us in the night. That one day there will be a change of worlds, and we must use everything that we possess to cross the threshold into a new earth.

There were some things that really stuck in my mind. I attended church even before I can remember. I knew of Christ, but I was amazed when White Eagle told me of the myth that Christ came to the white man first and he was killed for his trouble. The Messiah said he would return, and he had. First in Nevada and then he migrated and spread his word to the lands west of the Blackfoot, in the mountains and caves of the Glacier National Park. He was known to the Indians as the Messiah, the Wanekia ("one who makes live"), the Christ, as many believed, was called Wavoka.

He had heard a voice, which commanded him to travel to the south where the rivers run deep. He followed the voice to the village of Wavoka, where they met hundreds of other pilgrims of different tribes. All had come to meet the new Messiah.

"I have sent for you and am glad to see you," Wavoka said. "I am going to talk to you about your relatives that are dead and gone. My children, I want you to listen to all I have to say to you. I will teach you how to dance a dance, and I want you to dance it. Get ready for your dance, and when the dance is over, I will talk to you." We all danced the Ghost Dance during which many participants would faint or enter into a trance where they would see and speak to their dead relatives.

Wavoka spoke to his believers. He told them that there was another world coming, just like a cloud. It would come in a whirl-wind of the west and would crush out everything on this world "which was old and dying and that those who are at peace in their hearts already are in the great shelter of life. That there is no shelter for evil. In that other world, there was plenty of meat, just like old times, and in that world, all the dead Indians were alive, and all the bison that had ever been killed were roaming around again."

Wavoka also said, "The war that will bring on the new world will be a spiritual conflict with material matters. Material matters will be destroyed by spiritual beings who will remain to create one world and one nation under one power, that of the Creator. That time is not far off."

White Eagle then told us that Wavoka asked if he could travel with him where he would see a great flat valley near the great moun-tains on the way to the big water. A place where he could climb the mountaintops and live among the animals and eventually return to his father, the Great Spirit.

They set off back to the land of the Blackfoot knowing this was where Wavoka was speaking about. When they had reached the plains, White Eagle had given Wavoka the directions to access the summit. Wavoka told him, "I will leave my word in a black cave that sparkles in the mountains to bring light into the world. Whoever finds it will know it is a gift, and they must share it with others against the darkness of the other. Only when the time is right and with the right person will my world be with you and the others of the morning sun always." As he said that, the two parted ways.

The days before Willie and I were born, during the eclipse of the sun, Wavoka died and an eagle carried him to the sky. When he returned to earth, he was alive again and said he had a message from God. He said, "You must not hurt anybody or do harm to anyone. You must not fight. Do right always." The Indian nations never saw him again.

The Blackfeet believe that the caves were a holy place and protected them. That is why, even today, they find black soot and color their moccasins black.

We heard the story of Wavoka when we were very young and remembered it whenever we would go into the mountains to fish and hunt and play as kids do. My father, White Eagle, Willie, and I would fish the ice-cold streams for salmon during the summers and for deer and elk all year long. Not for sport but for food. There was bighorn sheep, mountain goats, and ptarmigan. We all rode horses into the mountains and across the plains. Life was exciting but dangerous; at the turn of the century, we would often see white and black grizzly bears and wolf packs in the mountains. Even though there were only a few whites in the reservation area, we were accepted as brothers. My Indian brothers taught me the understanding for all people.

My family and I lived in what the Blackfeet call the backbone of the world, the magnificent Rockies, which included the Glacier National Park, the "Crown of the Continental," which shares a border with Waterton Lakes National Park in Southern Alberta, Canada.

We could walk out our door and look to the left and see the Rockies. I could look to the right and see the plains with the cattle and horses grazing. I always thought it was the most beautiful place on earth.

I first became interested in archeology when I was about ten years old. Willie and I were playing on the reservation where an ancient river had flowed seventy-three million years ago. We saw a giant skull was sticking out of the rocks in the bed after a week of long rain. Quickly we went to tell Willie's father what we had found. He told us that there were many relics of ancient times on the reser-vation and they should stay in their resting place and we should not disturb them.

Several years later, I left the reservation and I found out that we had first seen the smallest and complete skeleton of a juvenile tyran-nosaur found in North America. The dinosaur was about three years of age when it died. The tyrannosaur was very closely related to the *Tyrannosaurus rex.*

Willie and I would often try to find the "cave that sparkles" growing up, but we never did. When I was seventeen, I was getting ready to run away to Canada to fight in World War I. The day before I had planned to leave, there was a giant earthquake in the mountains near the reservation. Willie was off the reservation with his father when the earthquake happened.

As I looked at the mountains when the earth stopped trem-bling, I heard the words "Seek and ye shall find." I went to the area again where the legend of the black caves spoke about. As I looked around, I found a small opening on the side of the mountain that wasn't there before, appearing because of the quake. I climbed into the opening, and it turned into a black cave.

When I turned on my torch, the cave turned in an amazing display of sparkling stars. I knew I had found the cave as described in the legend. I wandered down into the chasm. As I moved further into the cave, I stopped and rotated the light. The rest of the cave was blocked. There I saw a black medallion the length of my index finger. It had strange writing on it and a crystal in the middle of it. I left the cave and took the black medallion back to Willie's house. I had heard the legend of Wavoka and the black medallion. The medallion was believed to be thousands of years old that came beyond the stars and from the beginning of time.

I buried the medallion in a box under a corner of my father's barn. I left the next morning for Canada without speaking to Willie or his father. It was a secret that I only wanted to share with Willie. We had a pact, and I had hoped to see him soon when the war was over.

I joined the Royal Canadian Army and was sent to France to fight with the British regulars.

Finally, in 1920, World War I was over, and Europe would wait for the coming of the Third Reich.

I was discharged from the army. I didn't go back to Montana. I had seen much of the world when left after high school, and I wanted to see more and continue my education. I applied and was accepted to Princeton University studying archeology. This was my passion.

This is where I went on my first dig in Peru. I found a similar vibration between the discovering Inca artifacts and those I found with Willie on the Blackfoot reservation. The dig and the classes inspired me even more to find out about the past and the hidden meanings around us.

After graduation, I taught history at the all-girls school Wellesley College twelve miles west of Boston. For me, it was a great place to work and live. It was close to the museums and archeology centers of Boston and New York. I had great freedom to go around the world on digs. I became world-renowned for my discoveries in Mexico.

I eventually made it back to Princeton in 1930 to teach. In 1932, several colleagues and pupils from the arts and archeologist department and I were funded to go to Antioch. I was the field director for eight digging campaigns for the committee for the excavation of Antioch and its vicinity.

It was called the Lost Ancient City. It ranked with Rome, Alexandria, and Constantinople as one of the four great cities of the Roman and early Christian world, but it was the least known. It is located in southeastern Turkey near the border with Syria.

Its glory had vanished many centuries ago, and the loca-tion was now a modest Turkish town. It is fifteen miles from the Mediterranean on a navigable river, giving it great economic and strategic advantages.

The valley where Antioch was located produced favorable climatic conditions for agriculture, and the city was well supplied with grain, fresh produce, oil, and wines. Fed by springs, the city had abundant water, which was a source of pride and plea-sure for its inhabitants.

The city was founded in 300 BC and was settled by a large numbers of Greeks. The city was often compared to Athens. In the fourth-century AD, it had grown to be a vital metropolis set on the crossroads between the Euphrates river to the East and the ports of the Mediterranean to the west, and between Ephesus to the north and Jerusalem to the south.

The city had a middle class, and there seemed to be equality and abundance for all. The Roman emperor Julian called Antioch a "gay and prosperous city." It was rich in art, entertainment, and mosaics.

The city came under Roman control in 64 BC, and it became a Roman military center in the region.

Christianity was prosecuted until AD 312 when the emperor Constantine accepted the religion. From that time on, only Judaism and Christianity were accepted. All other religions were forbidden.

Several Christian strains flourished in the city. One Christian sect with dualistic and Gnostic elements was called the Cathari.

When Emperor Julian came to the Roman throne in AD 360, he threw aside the Christian faith and attempted to reestablish the big, or of polytheist, worship. The Christian church was too power-ful to be destroyed directly, but Julian took away much of its author-ity and tried to present a cogent alternative, "pagan church." This attempt failed completely, and the residents of Antioch were always seeking anything Christian to worship.

The city came under several Persian attacks, who captured and sacked the city. Several earthquakes destroyed almost the entire city.

After a major earthquake in AD 528, the city was named Theopolis, which means "City of God."

The city came under several Persians attacks who captured and sacked the city over several hundred years. In AD 637, the city was finally captured by the Persians, and the Christians had to flee toward Rome to save their lives.

My experiences in Antioch were many, and I had many professional successes. We unearthed many fantastic mosaics, wooden furniture, carved bones, statues, jewelry, and other items from the ancient city that are now in Paris and the Worcester Art Museum in Massachusetts, but success didn't come easy. By 1935, I was working on limited credit, and the digging was about to end because our actual findings did not meet the expectations of the committee's expectations. Then we discovered the "Boat of Psyches," depicting Eros in a chariot pulled by Psyches. This mosaic, as depicted by pagan legend, was the "Chariot of the Gods." Which Gods, I never did find out.

I became very familiar with the Middle East during the time that Hitler came to power in Germany. Our government became very concerned about the situation there and the anticipated need for oil in that region. So I was approached by the OSS to work as an operative under the guise of my work.

As the war loomed closer and closer, I had to work my diggers. I was always fair and thoughtful of those working with me on my quest to find out much as possible at the digging sites in Antioch. I had received approval during the summer of 1938 to hire several additional crews to help unearth the remaining artifacts of the Great Church, which was destroyed when the Persians sacked the city in AD 610. I found many artifacts I could identify and others that were very strange in nature. While I found mosaics, they have human images with creature features. Angels that were of the light and yet had eyes filled with darkness. During my venturing into the catacombs, I found tombs of skeletons that seemed to be of people that suffered from genetic defects. For some reason, when the artifacts and skeletons of the Great Church were sent to the Louvre in 1938, they never were displayed in the museum. All the other items recov-ered in Antioch can today be found there, but not them.

During the two summers of 1938 and 1939 excavations, I became friends with a local Antioch Christian merchant whose name was Murat. He had a huge house with many artifacts of his own that dated back to the time before Jesus. His family had lived in Antioch since they migrated from Jerusalem shortly after Christ died. His family had always been merchants and had their own ships. They had developed many alliances in Rome, Persia, and Egypt.

In 1939, my staff and I had been informed that we could no longer dig in the area. Murat asked me to have dinner with him and his family the night before I left and I agreed. After dinner, Murat asked me to come into his study so he could show me his private collection of family relics. I was surprisingly amazed. He showed me, as he believed, the nails that were driven into Christ's hands, the Key to Hayden, and a crystal from a ship from the heavens.

He told me he understood that all the items recovered from the digging sites belonged to the committee, but he had a gift that he was personally giving to me. He wanted me to respect that it was a gift from him to me, and it was not for the committee. I agreed. He then opened up a cabinet and took out a box made of gold that had two symbols on it. They were Christian symbols of water and fire. He took out the medallion that was shaped like fire and gave it to me. It was on a thin gold chain and was black. It looked remarkably like the one I found in Montana, except it was a different shape and it had unusual writing on it. That was just a fleeting thought. I put it on, thanked him, and went back to my hotel room to get ready to go back to Massachusetts.

During the war years, I spent more time working for the OSS than I did at the college. While in Iran in 1945, I met my wife, Martha, who was from Hungary. She had two boys, and her husband had been taken prisoner by the Soviets, where he had been working on the Iranian railroad. Her husband died while in captivity.

After the war, we spent time in Europe. Martha gave me a son named Edward. When he was five, I gave him the medallion that was given to me by Murat in Antioch. We shortly thereafter moved to the ranch I inherited in Montana. I remembered the medallion that I had hidden under the corner of the barn and, to my amazement, found it was still buried in the box from fifty something years ago. I also wore the medallion that was similar to Edward's. They both had very unusual writing on them. His carvings resembled fire and mine resembled water.

I had developed a very aggressive kind of skin cancer having been out in the sun on my digs for years. The doctors had told me that the cancer could be terminal. To my amazement, after I started wearing the medallion, the skin cancer went into remission, and I started to feel younger and stronger for the following twenty years.

We both went to see my old friend Willie Brightfeather on the reservation. He told me that his father, White Eagle, had passed a few years earlier, and he was now the chief of the tribe. He was now called Golden Eagle and had great medicine. As they sat outside in the cool air, I told Golden Eagle about finding the black medallion in the sparkling cave fifty years earlier. He then said, "Now I know why I couldn't find it! I never stopped looking for it." I showed it to him, and I also showed him Edward's, which he was wearing around his neck. He said to me, "You may be the beginning, but he is not the end." I did not know what he meant by that, but I was sure that there was more Indian legend that was connected with what he said. I vowed to return another day and talk to him further.

I noticed, or maybe it was my imagination, that Edward seemed to have really advanced academically after the age of five. So much so that we put him in a private school in Boston. He graduated from high school at age fourteen and college at sixteen. His advancement was mind-boggling. He had just been an average student until the age of five, when he started wearing his necklace twenty-four hours a day.

We spent time living both in Montana and Boston. We moved back to the Boston area permanently, where Edward attended Harvard and got his law degree. He did change in several ways. Some good, some bad. He certainly became smarter, was hardly sick, and almost became clairvoyant. He had little emotion toward me or his mother. He was almost cold-blooded.

*   *   *

At this point the notes stopped. I had to see and talk to her again. The next day I went to her house again.

Ethel told me that Henri stopped putting anything down in writing because he became concerned about his and Martha's well-being. The CIA, which was formally the OSS, were becoming interested in Edward in the 1960s and had visited Henri's house, asking about him. He knew then that their lives were going to change.

Ethel told me that she had met Edward's parents when they were married. She said that she had not met them earlier because of the strained relationship he had with them. Henri and Martha never really understood what happened between them and were very hurt and disappointed.

She grew very close to Henri when CHADD was born. He was in his seventies and was trying to make peace with himself and others in his life. He and Martha had moved back to the ranch in Montana that he had inherited when he retired. When he came east to see CHADD, he found time to be with her. Henri spent time with her at the hospital and told her more of the story of his life.

He then gave her the relic that he found in the sparkling black cave. He asked her to give it to CHADD when she thought it was the right time.

Ethel told me she had a doctor's appointment and she really couldn't talk any longer. So we said our goodbyes, and I started to think about all the things I had learned.

Becoming Their
Human Lab Test

E thel started to describe to me all the medications and tests that
she was aware of that CHADD had been subjected to between
the ages of five to eighteen. I was shocked to hear of all the
drugs that were put into his body. CHADD's medical records showed
Ethel the drugs and the effects of those drugs. The records stated the
following:

- Risperdal—For irritability. Did not seem to help. He had
  been on higher doses, and it doesn't seem to do anything to
  manage the irritability. First two weeks were good and then
  after that, nothing.
- Lamictal—For mood swings. Dose now is very low because
  it hadn't had much effect. Dexedrine Spansule tablet didn't
  help.
- Ritalin—For weight loss, anxiety, and depression. He was so
  anxious, he would vomit. He would see a cloud coming and
  run looking for cover for fear that lightning was going to hit
  him.
- Cylert Adderall—Helped for first week and then it made him
  depressed.

- Serzone—Didn't seem to help.
- Effexor—Didn't seem to help. Increased aggression and defiance.
- Neurontin—Didn't seem to help and seemed to make things worse.
- Mellaril—Mild sedating effect, but didn't seem to help other than to sedate him a little.
- Remeron—Didn't do anything. Was used to help him sleep, but then it caused him to sleep too much.
- Catapres—It helped for two weeks in making him more cooperative.

He was also prescribed lithium for two weeks, which didn't do anything and Wellbutrin SR. Both are very toxic and made him very sick. His medication regimen was evaluated every six weeks by psychotherapists for seven years. Numerous tests had been done over the years as he was growing up. These included brain SPECT studies, Connor CPR, etc. The brain SPECT test showed increased left and right medical temporal lobe activity, increased left and right inferior prefrontal cortex activity, and increased anterior cingulated activity.

Ethel had seen the psychiatric diagnoses over the years of ADHD, insomnia, delusions, motor tics, depression, oppositional defiant disorder, ADD, bipolar disorder, and central auditory pro-cessing problems. Ethel did not believe in the high concentration of drugs were necessary for CHADD to think clearly and function properly on a day-to-day basis. CHADD could not endure this con-stant foggy state any longer. CHADD said, "I wish I was dead." Ethel thought love, natural remedies, and therapy would help CHADD grow out of his childhood issues. One thing that the doctors and Ethel agreed upon was that the drugs had many side effects and cre-ated more problems than they solved.

Ethel had seen firsthand how prescription drugs were affecting society and everyone in it. She noted more people with prescription drug addictions were in treatment centers than those that used illegal drugs. The number of admissions for prescription drug abuse had more than quadrupled in the last decade. In 1998, the largest group of women admitted for prescription drug abuse treatment in Florida was age 26 to 45. Today the largest group is 21 to 30. The drugs used by these women are often oxycodone, Vicodin, methadone, and Xanax.

Young women are using antidepressants and anti-anxiety drugs during pregnancy. Combined with a "safe drug" like alcohol, not only are more babies born with withdrawal symptoms but also more birth defects and mental impairments are being noted as they age. Even babies are now suffering from the use by their mother's during pregnancy. The withdrawal patterns seem to be worse with prescription drugs than what is typically seen with heroin. The worst noted have been with mothers that had been on Xanax and methadone.

Being in the health-care field, Ethel was adamant that most of the drugs being used by people are disconnecting them to their higher self and that we are becoming less responsive to them. The viruses are building up tolerances to the drugs and are now being called super-bugs that resist everything thrown at them. They are known as staph infections that often require body tissue to be removed so that the person can live. The irony is that the staph infections are found in hospitals. She knew it was because the bugs' adept to the medications and becoming stronger if they live through the initial contact with the medications. She often questioned why blood was being drawn from CHADD at abnormal levels and why she was asked to sign legal documents for a special DNA test when he was five. To her, his treatment was highly irregular, but she knew CHADD had symp-toms of extreme uneasiness.

Ethel knew most of CHADD's issues were real; he was always different. Even before he was born, he would have times of extreme activity and then times of no activity at all. They became very apparent starting at the age of two. Ethel also told me that his memory was fantastic and that he never got sick. He would often appear to know what she was thinking. When she would ask him why he was acting the way that he was at school and getting bad grades, he said, "I am bored and I know everything they are talking about already. I don't belong there."

As he grew older, she knew exactly what he meant.

Light, Sound, and Drugs

E ven before we met, I had been involved with Light and Sound therapy, as well as researching prescription drugs and their effects on people. It all began when my cousin was diagnosed with cancer five years after her aunt had breast cancer and a couple of years after her uncle was diagnosed with terminal cancer. The list goes on with three other members of my relatives with Alzheimer's. God told me how to release it with the light in three minutes from the body when CHADD had two months left with Alzheimer's due to the many drugs he'd had.

There is one disease and it is chaos at the atomic (atom) and cellular level, which is the molecular level. When the cells are in "chaos," you feel it through symptoms in the body. Symptoms means that it is a signal that there is chaos and of course its discomfort. Disease comes from discomfort, and there are only two things that cause it at the molecular level.

One that is *toxicity* and the other is *deficiency*. And when you have symptoms of discomfort, you most probably have both. But you see there is not a single prescription over the counter of a pre-scription drug that does not create a bigger toxicity and bigger chaos leading to cellular unbalance and other effects of which they call side effect so people don't take it seriously.

We are holographic bodies of light and we resonate at a frequency. We are mainly water and energy. We have an etheric body, an aura and vortex of energy called chakras. Light therapy is a natural medicine that restores that the body's needs without the harmfulness of chemical products of the drugs. The therapy is gently given and not forced into the digestive tract, the blood, or the tissues. It does not directly affect the organs, but it restores the balance of the body at the level of the etheric (aura) but also rebalance the vortex of energy that are called chakras, at which time the health is reestablished.

Although approved by the FDA, prescription drugs are still drugs and many of them have important side effects, the purpose of the most-known prescribed drugs is supposed to be to cure, so it should not take a lifetime to ingest. These prescribed drugs damage more than they cure. They require other prescriptions to counteract the effect of the side effects. It is a vicious circle. In the world of illegal drugs, far too many people die from prescription drugs than from illegal drugs. Each drug is artificially and chemically based and a source of big profits to the manufacturer. Often drug representatives leave samples when they call on doctors. They have often given doctors incentives to prescribe their medications.

An herb is a natural plant that still maintains its natural properties, which remain untouched. There is a prescription epidemic where many babies are born addicted to antidepressants and anti-anxiety drugs during pregnancy. "Babies are suffering from withdrawal patterns, and it seems to be worse (with prescription drugs) than what we were with heroin," says Dr. Terri Ashmeade, medical director of Tampa General Hospital's neonatal intensive care unit. When a pregnant mother tries to stop cold turkey, the unborn baby could have seizures and die.

Many of the illnesses unexplained today can be related to ingestion of drugs. One relieves certain symptoms and often creates other side effects, thus needing more prescription drugs. It can be a never-ending cycle and sometimes creates a downward spiral that causes death. The medicine, by colors, when applied correctly has no side effects because they do not address the symptoms but get to the cause directly where the energy has been cut. In offering the supplement in the body through the light, the body chooses what it needs and the quantity it needs.

Contemporary medicine is used to treat symptoms only on the physical level. Surgery and medications very often only treat the symptom without curing the problem. One must understand why surgery and prescription drugs often slow down or sometimes inhibit the person from healing. To successfully rebalance the energy, the cause of all illnesses, the technique of the forty-ninth vibration begins at the highest vibratory levels (etherics).

The color light is based on a concept of a chemical unbalance, a state of illness, and energy of vibration that needs to be corrected in the body. The base of illness starts when the energy of the aura changes color. The alternative medicine by color contrasts with the orthodox medicine. The body actually absorbs the light and reacts to the light in photosynthesis. When the energy is absorbed, its level is raised before soon returning to its normal state. All illnesses, at their initial state, are attributed to the imbalance of the etheric fields or to the health of the aura at the energy level. The medical profession also uses light therapy, but they only confine themselves to the use of infrared or ultraviolet light. This can be harmful because it is out of the beneficial range visible to the human eye.

Sound frequencies of low intensity and acoustic energy can induce strong effects on human behavior. Sound and light are forms of resonant vibrations that change the human brain and body. However, subtle energy, harmonic frequencies, rapidly balance and restore the natural energies of your body and mind. This improves memory, creativity, learning, and intelligence.

Our five senses drive our day-to-day existence. If the light is just right or the sound just so, it could trigger a new sense of aware-ness to another sense of reality. There is a direct correlation between the light frequency and the mind's ability to see what is not there! In addition to sound, light can cause someone to perceive images, intricate patterns, shapes, and colors. Light is a big part of the book of knowledge.

The military have been working on secret projects that involve Light and Sound—how they affect enemy troops and how the human body responds to stimuli.

My study of prescription drugs was very revealing to me. Look closer at the actual social context in which we live concerning these "wonderful" substances. Those that are on a spiritual path very quickly learn that what we leave out of our brains, our bodies, and our spirit is as important as what we put inside it. In reality, the war against drugs is not really a war against drugs, but a very small part among thousands of medications approved by the FDA. Prescription drugs are still drugs, and many of them have important side effects. The purpose of the most known prescribed drugs is supposed to be to cure. These prescribed drugs sometimes damage more than they cure and require other prescription to counteract the effect of the side effects. It is a vicious circle. In the world of legal drugs, far too many persons die from prescribed drugs than from illegal drugs.

A complaint was submitted to the International Criminal Court at The Hague on June 14, 2003. The complaint brought before the court states crimes perpetrated by the pharmaceutical "business with disease" to

1. Maintain cardiovascular diseases, including high blood pressure, heart failure, diabetic complications, and other diseases, cancer, infectious diseases including AIDS, osteoporosis, and many other of today's most common diseases that are recognized to be largely preventable by natural means and caused the unnecessary suffering and prema-ture death of millions of people.
2. Prevent the eradication of cardiovascular disease, cancer, and other diseases by obstructing and blocking the dis-semination of life-saving information on the health bene-fits of natural nonpatentable therapies.
3. Expand existing diseases and creating new diseases. Specific evidence was presented that today's most common diseases are deliberately maintained and expanded, despite the fact that

these diseases could have been effectively prevented and largely eradicated—saving millions of lives. Some pharmaceutical drugs flush out essential nutrients from the body, thereby aggravating the underlying cause of the disease.

Punta Cayenna

E thel had tears running down her face as she told me how her
son was deceived and taken to an abusive boot camp in Punta
Cayenna at fourteen years old.

CHADD had acted up and defied his stepmother's order to clean
up his room. He would talk back to her and would slam his bedroom
door. He screamed at her and told her that he would rather die than
do what she said anymore. Katherine used this as a great opportunity
to have CHADD committed. She had spoken to Edward several
times over the years since they had been married to place him in a
center away from them and Ethel.

A few weeks later Edward, Katherine, CHADD, and Paul went
on a family vacation. They flew into Punta Cayenna and stayed at
a well-known resort there. On the seventh day of their vacation,
Edward told CHADD that they were going to look at a school while
they were there. They drove from the north side of the island down
near Frenchman's Bay. There was a complex there that used to be
a hotel, a Catholic Church retreat, then it was owned by the US
Army. It was then a behavior modification center, which charged over
$40,000 a year to "cure" the students. It was run through ICHANGE
(International Center Home's Angels), a group that is operated out
of Salt Lake City, Utah. ICHANGE has several facilities around
the world. Edward and CHADD arrived at the facility to find a

white twenty-foot wall surrounding the grounds. It looked serene, a white sandy beach across the street with a multitude of palm trees in the area. They walked into the front office and sat down with Mr. Jones. Mr. Jones welcomed both of them. Mr. Jones then asked for CHADD's "brothers" to come into the room. To CHADD's amazement, they were huge Punta Cayennans that had the responsibility to watch and restrain teens when necessary.

Mr. Jones then told Edward and CHADD that CHADD may not like the daily routine, but that it would make him a better person. CHADD was escorted to his new home away from home by his two new brothers.

Edward then signed a legal contract with Mr. Jones that gave him 49 percent custody rights. By giving the school the custody rights, the school was given the right to use whatever physical force they felt necessary to control the teens. He also gave him a check for $3,500 for the first month, totally excluding Ethel from any parental rights at all. Mr. Jones discussed the procedures in place for visitation and contact with CHADD. There was no visitation or contact allowed for six months. That would give the school time to modify the behavior of the student. Also, each parent would have to go through three seminars stateside so they would understand the "program" and how the students would try to manipulate them to taking them out of the school. Mr. Jones told Edward the procedure of giving him the drugs that are prescribed for him. His family "father" would monitor his prescription drug use and would make sure he took them. CHADD also felt that other drugs were given to the students unknowingly to control them, but he couldn't prove it. He certainly had no one to tell of his beliefs; he thought his food had concentrations of drugs. The other members of his "family" would act irrational and extremely sullen at times. CHADD knew that this is not how they really were; something must have been given to them.

Each group either male or female had around twenty students. They would sleep in one big room and could not speak, go to the bathroom, or read unauthorized material without the permission of each "father" or "mother." The boys could not look at the girls and vice versa. If they did, they would go into what was called OP or observation placement.

This was known as "lying on your face." Guards would take them to a small bare room and make them lie flat on their face, arms by their sides, on the tiled floor. Watched by a guard, they must remain lying face down, forbidden to speak or move a muscle except for ten minutes every hour, when they could sit up and stretch before resuming the position. Meals were brought to them, and at night they slept on the floor of the corridor outside under electric light and watched by a guard. At dawn they would do the same thing again. At times when taken to OP, the guards would stretch out the student and step on their ankles, grinding them into the tile.

The facility was more like a brainwashing prison than anything else. The only way to leave was to reach a reward and punishment to affect change. To graduate or leave the school, a student had to advance from level 1 to level 5 by earning points. As a student accumulated higher scores, he or she would progress from level to level and acquire privileges. As a student got to levels 4, 5, or 6, they were employed for three days a week as a member of the staff and would have to discipline other students by issuing consequences. They basically became guards themselves by telling on their friends and other students.

CHADD found this unethical and cruel. He refused to tell on his friends and other students and would often go back to level 1 and go to OP. He once was in OP for six months because he wouldn't tell on his friend Marco, whom he met the first day. Edward dropped him off with the deception of "It's a school right on the beach. You'll love it."

When CHADD was dropped off at the school, he was fourteen and 120 pounds. He didn't weigh much or grow in height when he left right after he turned seventeen. He ate fish and cabbage every morning for breakfast and pork every night. Sometimes the pork still had skin and hair on it. It made him sick at first, but he found out that he had to eat at least half of it. Even if he ate all the food they gave him, he was always hungry.

CHADD's first and only friend was Marco, a kid from Boca Raton who coincidently only lived a short distance from CHADD's home. He was fourteen and the two boys really got along well. There were differences in their personalities and the reasons they were in Serenity Bay. Marco knew how to work the system, operate under the radar, be accepted by adults, play them like a violin, and even get away with murder. He was there because he was dealing drugs at fourteen at school, and one of his customers gave some of the drugs to a friend that overdosed. That could never be proven by the police, but since Marco's father was a prominent politician, the father was given the advice that Marco had been under surveillance for quite some time and that there were rumors on the street about him. The police chief, a close friend who also headed up the death investigation, suggested sending him away for a while in a controlled environment that would not impact his reelection. No politician needs a fourteen-year-old drug dealer son on the streets—wouldn't look good to the voters. A proactive father would. The death never was reported in the papers, and no one other than the police chief knew that Marco was the main suspect.

Marco and CHADD had arrived within days of each other at the center. Neither boy changed during their stays at the center. Marco returned to Florida in a little less than two years, and CHADD returned after three years. While at the center, Marco made friends with a guard. Learning by watching his father work other people, Marco made a deal with the guard to get special privileges and would promise the guard items that he would request from the "care packages" his parents would send him. Since the guard was the one monitoring the packages, everything worked well for him for a while. Marco liked smoking marijuana and the guard liked US dollars. Marco was a bragger and liked to show off which often got him in trouble in the center. CHADD was defiant and that got him in trouble.

CHADD knew about what Marco was up to. One day the guard that usually watched CHADD's group was out sick. A new guard noticed a half-smoked joint near CHADD's bed that had been dropped by Marco on his way out of the room where they all lived and slept. Mr. Jones immediately suspected CHADD because he had a reputation of always being difficult and defiant. He looked guilty. Three guards grabbed him and took him to OP. They asked where the joint came from, but he refused to talk. He had his ankles ground into the tile and had to lay face down for six months because he would not talk and tell them where the drugs came from. His rep-utation changed at the center. He was now someone who could be trusted and could not be broken; he would become like a hero. This hardened him and made him even angrier than before.

CHADD's mother had used all of her resources including her retirement funds, and she filed bankruptcy. She still was unable to get CHADD released from the school. She said that his new wife, Katherine, created all the legal battling with Edward. Katherine wanted to destroy Ethel and she basically succeeded. The day after the court decided in Edward's favor, he alone could put CHADD in Punta Cayenna and keep him there.

Edward took him out. Katherine's mission was accomplished, destroying Ethel and leaving her with nothing. Ethel's emotional and mental damage was very obvious to me. She was very emotional, had been on prescription drugs for years, was always paranoid, and when-ever we would speak about CHADD, she would pour herself a glass of red wine and would continue drinking even after I left her house.

During this time together, I asked her how she knew all these things. She told me she found out through discovery in her lawsuit with Edward, speaking with CHADD when he returned, and with other parents at the seminars. The other parents had been through the misery and deception of ICHANGE. The parents would protest and would try to tell the new parents attending the seminars that Punta Cayenna was a hell for the kids and a place of abuse. They then were escorted away from the seminar by police at the urging of ICHANGE.

She took a moment to compose herself after talking about Edward's deception and the years she fought for CHADD where she lost everything, including her mind. She continued on.

CHADD was one of 250 males and females at the facility. He was like several others who were defiant and oppositional. He never harmed anyone or himself. He was bored at school and at home and just didn't fit in with anyone.

Others at the school were violent, had dealt drugs, used drugs, and had committed crimes. Although a court did not order the kids to this facility, their parents sent their troubled teens to centers around the world, including this one, out of sight and out of mind. Ethel needed to pour herself another drink before she could continue her story.

She told me that at first, she was furious with Edward about dropping CHADD off at the school. She had no idea what was going on, and it was against the child custody agreement that they had signed. Edward assured her that it was the only way to help him. He sent her videotapes of the facility, testimonials from other parents and ex-students, and a very glossy brochure. She still did not buy into what he had done.

When she asked for the phone number so she could call CHADD, she was told that she couldn't talk to CHADD for six months or see him for a year. At that point, she had to go to three seminars, costing $1,000 each, to learn how to work with the facility to modify CHADD's behavior. She was furious but had no other choice. She attended her first, and as she walked up to the hotel where the seminar was being held, she saw the demonstrators yelling, "Save your children. Don't listen to them. They are evil." She became very frightened for CHADD after hearing those words. She con-tinued into the large meeting room with almost five hundred other parents and ex-students.

She sat next to a doctor and his wife and listened to their story. They had been told by a behavior consultant that the group of behavior modification centers were the best and largest in the coun-try. Later she would find out that he was a paid consultant and that he would receive money from both the parents and ICHANGE. He was actually populating the centers with children that ICHANGE had outlined they wanted at their centers. The doctor told her that they had a daughter that was always in trouble. They did everything they could but could not control her. So in the middle of the night, two approved escorts came to their house, handcuffed their daughter, put her in a van, and then she was flown to Punta Cayenna. They were sad and upset at first but believed it was the best thing for their fourteen-year-old daughter.

The seminar began and everyone was told that they could not leave the seminar for any reason for the next eight hours, even for an emergency. Ethel saw more videos of all the ICHANGE centers and listened to testimonials from parents who had children return happy and under control. She heard testimonials from former students that said their center changed their life. The head of the ICHANGE, Robert Mundi, the president's brother, also spoke about how a life-changing experience this will be for the students. For the parents, they would not have to struggle with their children any longer. When they arrived home, they would be appreciative and thankful for what they had.

Ethel thought this was just too unbelievable for her. Some stayed for the entire seminar to see just what they were saying and speak to other people. Most of the parents in the room seemed to be very supportive. She noticed another woman who seemed to be very uncomfortable with what was being said on stage and the marketing package being presented to everyone.

The other woman's name was Edith. Edith told Ethel that a girl had jumped to her death the day after she arrived at Punta Cayenna. The police found no wrongdoing. Bars were installed, and it didn't look like a school but a prison. She said the school didn't have any other reported events to the police because the island made money from the facility. The island not only received funds from the school but also from the US government. She noted that most students had returned to their parent's home and were void of feelings, emotions, would have terrible nightmares, and would wake up screaming in the middle of the night. Also, ICHANGE would pay the parents and the students. If a parent referred other parents to the centers, they would get a month's free tuition.

Edith told Ethel that if she really loved her son, to get him back in the US where at least there was monitoring of living conditions and if the kids were being abused. She also said that the government was involved, and she still may not have much control of her son's destiny.

Ethel had heard enough and thanked Edith. Between what Edith said and what she heard at the seminar, she flew home the next day and told Edward she wanted to speak to him immediately.

Edward and Ethel met at a Cuban café in Miami. When she told him of the seminar and what Edith had said, he dismissed it as another fanatical anti-government conspiracy nutcase making up stories. He had been to the center, been to the seminar, and spoke to other parents and ex-students. He had no problem with it at all. Ethel knew that the one who was OK with it was really Katherine. She wanted her son away from both Edward and Ethel for her own reasons, which Ethel could never figure out.

After the meeting with Edward, she knew that he would never yield and bring CHADD home. That is when the long road of anguish, pain, and despair would start. Years of loving and missing her son, legal battles, years of trying to get CHADD home, and sinking deeper and deeper into the abyss of misery.

To her, Edward would always be a liar and a cheat. He cheated his son out of four years of his childhood and time with his mother and father. Things Ethel would never forgive nor would CHADD. The twig had been bent, so now grows the tree.

Another Day

CHADD had gone back to his house, and I could not reach him for days. My life had changed by that chance meeting in the coffee shop. The one person that I thought could help me reach him was his mom. So I went to see her.

I remembered his mother had told me that she had more to tell me. I waited a couple of days to let my thoughts settle and to try to understand what I had gotten into. Whatever it was, it was different than anything I had known before.

I parked in Ethel's driveway and walked up to the door before I went to my office. I rang the doorbell. Once again, she looked out of the window and slowly opened the front door. I told her I was back to hear more about CHADD's life because I was concerned about him, and she let me in. The German shepherd followed us into the living room and laid down next to her.

She was very hospitable and again offered me some tea. I agreed and we started to talk. She had much to say. A lot of things I thought were very unusual and hard to believe, but I gave her the courtesy and listened, only occasionally asking questions.

She started by telling me that Edward was very handsome and very intelligent. She knew he was the one the moment she met him during a football tailgate party. He had a birthmark on the top of his right hand that looked like a cross, but she was not repelled by that at all. She also noticed that while most people she knew wore a crucifix or a star of David around their neck, Edward wore a black medallion that was a gift from his father—that he found on one of his many excavations in the Middle East.

She told me that she had married CHADD's father, Edward, when she graduated from college, and Edward was several years out of law school. He had already started working as a government attor-ney. The school was in Northern Florida and had hills and even a change in seasons. They both loved it especially during football sea-son, when they would attend the games with their friends. She had a special relationship with Edward's father who had taught at Wesley and was a world-renowned archeologist. She was the only girl in the family, and Edward was the only child to his parents, Henri and Martha. Ethel's parents had passed several years earlier in a car acci-dent. Ethel felt she had a family again when she was with Edward and his family. Martha treated her like a daughter, and she loved that.

Ethel was finishing up her senior year of college while Edward was working for the government. He told her that he could never go into details. That is where she felt the walls first went up and the secrets began.

Edward was working his job at the federal building in Miami three months before Ethel graduated. She was finishing her classes, packing and waiting for her new life to begin. Edward had found a small house a block from the beach in Coral Springs that, Ethel agreed, was perfect for their first house and where they could start a family. It was a short drive for Edward.

Ethel entered a nursing school. Health care was always her pas-sion, and she was very influenced by her father, who had been a doctor when he was alive.

Henri had given Ethel his medallion on a visit when he and Martha came to the house when CHADD was twelve. Even though Ethel was not married to Edward any longer, Ethel still had a rela-tionship with Martha. Henri had told Ethel the history of the medal-lion and its healing and positive-changing qualities. He wanted her to keep the medallion near CHADD at all times, and she was very willing to do so. Edward didn't have any problem with his father's gift for CHADD since it came from his father. He really liked it that his father gave it to his son.

CHADD was a very sensitive child. He was difficult to disci-pline and to parent, even before he started kindergarten. Edward had him tested when he was five years old.

From that time on, CHADD had been on multiple medications. Ethel could not tolerate her son being given drugs at such a young age. That was the primary reason that she and Edward divorced. She felt that CHADD was being used as a guinea pig, one drug after another to control his behavior. CHADD had a great memory and was very musical, but he just didn't fit into society and was difficult for everyone in his life, even his mother. She was dedicated to him and would not desert him.

Ethel started to tell me that she started doing drugs for her own depression and anxiety. With Edward's coaching and the doc-tor's urging at the government hospital, she soon became addicted to the drugs and her behavior became more and more erratic. When Edward and Ethel went to court for their divorce, Edward depicted Ethel as an unfit mother and a drug addict to the court. Edward was awarded primary custody.

A year before Ethel asked for a divorce, she found out that Edward had been having an affair with a coworker named Katherine, that he had started the affair when she was pregnant with CHADD. She blamed herself for the disintegration of their marriage even though she knew that it all centered around how Edward was treat-ing CHADD. As time went on and the legal bills kept increasing, Ethel became more depressed and was driven to more and stronger drugs. As much as she tried to hold her life together for her son, she couldn't do it. Edward was being brainwashed by Katherine, and she was doing everything possible to make herself look good and Ethel as a severely mentally ill person.

Ethel did admit to me that she had attempted to commit sui-cide twice—the first time when she found out about Edward's affair, the second when the courts awarded primary custody to Edward. All she had done, since he was born, was take care of CHADD and try to help him work through his problems. Through the years, she was put on Adderall, Ativan, Depakote, Valium, and several other medications. Most of the time these medications made her issues even worse, especially when she would drink red wine. Many times she felt she was losing her mind.

She just knew if she were to go to rehabilitation or to actually commit suicide, no one would be there for CHADD. She felt that she could not leave him no matter what.

Ethel then found a house very close to where CHADD lived and exercised her visitation rights. Because of her mental state, the visits were supervised for the first two years. The courts eventually allowed her to see CHADD on her own. She was supposed to share in parental decisions that concerned medical treatment and his education. Ethel could see that the drugs were affecting her young son more and more every visit. CHADD was now ten and had been on drugs since he was five.

For the first couple of years after the divorce, Edward first seemed to be sympathetic, but when he married Katherine, things changed. Edward became more and more distant from Ethel. He was unwilling to discuss CHADD more and more. Ethel believed that Katherine was behind the change in Edward, like she was making the decisions and not Edward.

CHADD was also having a hard time coping with Katherine's son, Paul. Paul was the same age as CHADD. Katherine tried to alienate Ethel and CHADD as much as possible over the years. She wouldn't let CHADD talk to his mom on the phone, wouldn't have him ready or say he was ill for visitation, tell CHADD that his mother didn't want to see him, and tell him that his mother stole his college funds from him. Katherine also told him that his mother was also mentally ill, a drug addict, and couldn't be trusted.

When CHADD told his mother what Katherine was saying about her, she spiraled even deeper into despair.

As time went on, Ethel became more and more dependent on her medications. The doctor who was prescribing the drugs kept telling her that she was making progress even when Ethel said she felt worse and worse. She became more and more withdrawn, and CHADD was becoming more and more difficult to be around.

CHADD had gone to Ethel's house for his visitation, the day that Henri gave his mother the medallion. When his mother gave it to him, he felt an energy that he had never felt before. He told her that it really felt good, but it kind of threw him a little off balance. Little did anyone know that the medallion was tuned into CHADD and Henri's spiritual frequencies and that only the two of them could feel its power.

Back to Dad's House

CHADD and I met a few days after I had spoken to Ethel about Punta Cayenna. I asked him about it, but he told me he blocked everything that happened there out of his mind.

As much as he tried, he could not articulate the pain and extreme anger that he experienced there.

He told me the day after his mom had lost her legal battle to bring him home, his father brought him back to the States. He couldn't believe how quickly it all happened. When he asked his father what made him bring CHADD home, his father told him because he found out the real conditions that CHADD was living under and didn't want his son being treated that way.

Edward picked CHADD up at the airport on Saturday, slightly after lunch. Katherine was not with him; CHADD was told that she was sick and couldn't make it. CHADD never did get along with her, so he was glad she was unable to come to pick him up.

CHADD was not the son that Edward expected to see. Even though CHADD had seen him six months earlier on the island, the staff had inflicted payback on CHADD before his release date. CHADD could hardly walk due to the grinding of his ankles into the tile during OP. CHADD had spent the last month on his face in OP and was given only half of the commonly deficient portions of food. He barely weighed 120 pounds and had a scary blank stare in his eyes. His head was shaven bald and his face was emotionless. He didn't start any conversation on the way back to the house.

He wasn't allowed to talk about Punta Cayenna, and he maintained all the rules and survival techniques that he learned in the behavior modified center. His behavior certainly was modified, but he was now full of hate and anger.

Arriving at the house, he was not greeted by Katherine or his half brother, Paul. Edward walked him to the same room he had four years earlier. Everything was left as if nothing had happened. CHADD asked if he could take a nap, and Edward understood and left him alone. CHADD slept through dinner and didn't wake until the next morning. Edward told CHADD to get dressed and they would go get something to eat and then go to the mall and walk around.

During breakfast, CHADD ordered pancakes, but he could only eat a couple of bites. His stomach had shrunk, and even though he wanted to eat, he couldn't. People in the restaurant would gaze at him like he was a criminal, which he never was. He was emotionally scarred, and those scars were apparent in his mannerisms and actions.

They arrived at the mall and started walking around. For the first time in four years, he could look at girls but did not know how to handle it. He had learned zero skills talking to women growing up. The thought of talking to a girl scared him. He was afraid of how he would act—the rejection he would feel.

They drove home for Sunday dinner. It was the first time CHADD had seen Katherine and Paul. Katherine didn't even recog-nize him as being there. Paul showed a genuine interest and was glad to see him.

Dinner was very touchy. No one knew how to interact with CHADD, and he was used to not talking during meals, just listening to the brainwashing tapes that he would listen to at Punta Cayenna. He went to his room after dinner and was told he would see his mom the next day.

CHADD met Ethel outside the next morning when she came to pick him up. She was so glad to have him home but was shocked in his appearance and how he acted. He stayed with her the next couple of days. They were both in anguish over how to act around each other. She started to talk to him about his time away. He could hardly speak and she could tell it was very painful for him. She chose her words wisely and would stop if she could tell he didn't want to talk about things. She wanted him to enjoy his time home and not pressure him.

Ethel fell even deeper in self-blame and depression after being around CHADD for a few days. At night, after CHADD had gone to sleep, Ethel started to drink even more with her prescription drugs. She blamed herself for what happened to her son. On Wednesday when Edward came to the house to pick up CHADD, Ethel sank even deeper into depression.

CHADD's life wasn't any better when he got back to Edward's house. He was still defiant and oppositional. Katherine didn't like him there and wanted him gone. Katherine called Edward, frantically saying she was afraid of CHADD. He had cursed her out when she asked him to clean up his room. She had provoked him by criticizing him and telling him that she wished he was back at Serenity Bay where he belonged. When Edward came home from work, she told him that CHADD needed to go into a halfway house to acclimate back into society. CHADD told him what happened, but Edward didn't believe him. Katherine convinced him otherwise. He agreed that he had to go away. A center was found in Birmingham, Alabama. It was not associated with ICHANGE; it was a military school. When Edward called Ethel this time, Ethel knew he was right. He did need a place to go until he was eighteen. A military school environment would provide structure and would be good for him, she thought. It was half a day's ride to see him. Edward told her that she could talk to him every weekend and see him every two weeks. This time he wasn't lying to her.

She wondered why he wasn't put in this facility to start with. Deep inside she really knew, Katherine intended to destroy her and to put CHADD someplace that was out of view. On both counts she would be right.

Edward drove CHADD to Alabama a month after he returned from Punta Cayenna. Edward hoped that CHADD would benefit from his almost a year stay in Alabama and would be helped to acclimate back into society.

Edward saw traits in CHADD's makeup that he had seen before and some new ones. CHADD seemed to be very knowledgeable about many things even though he had been away for four years, didn't watch any TV, listen to any radio, or have anything to read. He had to have developed a "sixth sense" about things—sometimes even reading Edward's mind. When Edward asked CHADD how he knew so many things, CHADD told him that people would come to him when he was in OP or he would "astro travel" to places on earth or on other worlds. Edward considered this to be hallucinations and CHADD's way of dealing with the conditions at Punta Cayenna. He even called it post-traumatic stress syndrome. Edward authorized bimonthly examinations and taking of blood for evaluation. He knew Ethel wouldn't approve of that invasive procedure, so he simply did not tell her. When she would call and talk to the medical staff, she never asked about it. She knew that CHADD was never sick in his entire life, and it would be very unusual for him to be ill while at the academy. The ride, for the most part, was uneventful.

They rented a room when they got into Birmingham, ate din-ner, and went to bed. The next morning, they pulled into the Paul E. Lee Military Academy between the city and Highway 20. Edward and CHADD met the school administrator, General Bledsoe. Things went smoothly and CHADD had a lot better feeling about this place than in Punta Cayenna. Edward left and CHADD went to his dorm. This was certainly more of a real-life experience well as structured. Even Ethel, when she visited, liked the place.

It was up to CHADD to take his own medications, a bad plan by Edward. Over a few months, both Edward and Ethel noticed more irritability and anxiety in their visits and phone calls. CHADD also noticed he had less control of his emotions especially his rage and anger. He was also having more visions and hearing more voices. He was not afraid or concerned about the visions or the voices. He knew, however, that he should not mention those things to the acad-emy psychiatrist or his parents. If he did, they would force him to take the drugs to control him. In his mind, he had to get away from all the things that contributed to his pain.

For a two-month period, neither Edward nor Ethel could see or speak to CHADD. General Bledsoe told each one of them that CHADD had disobeyed orders. Considering CHADD's past behavior, neither one of them questioned that information. CHADD spent almost a year at the academy.

He was now eighteen. He went back to Miami and decided to move in with his mother. For the first two weeks, he slept, listened to music, and watched TV. Ethel did not push him to do anything else, but she knew he couldn't do those things the rest of his life. Ethel worked with him to schedule his GED test, a test that he passed without any effort. Intelligence and knowledge were not his prob-lem. Living in the real world was. CHADD applied to many jobs, fast-food restaurants, gas stations, and amusement parks. He was accepted to work in the photo shop at Water World. He would take photos of people in the park, develop them, and if people wanted to buy them, process their purchase. Ethel enjoyed driving him to work and picking him up every day. It gave them time to talk. One afternoon Ethel received a phone call from CHADD. He informed her that he lost his job because a customer was being rude to him and he wasn't going to put up with it. The park found his actions and attitude as being rude.

CHADD then started working at a local big-box electronics store. He was always on time, but he often had words with his ware-house manager on how to do things. He didn't last long there either.

His mother had come to her wit's end. She called Edward and asked if he could do something with CHADD. She asked if he could move back to his dad's house. With hesitation, Edward gingerly asked Katherine. To his amazement, she agreed to allow CHADD to move back to the house without resistance. Edward didn't want to rock the boat, so CHADD moved back to his house. Paul had moved out before CHADD came back from Alabama, so it was just CHADD, Edward, and Katherine living there now. When CHADD and Edward got back to the house, Edward gave him back his black medallion that he had removed from him years earlier before he went to Punta Cayenna. CHADD felt the energy from it again and felt stronger and his head clearer for the first time in years.

After a couple of days of listening to music, watching TV, and sleeping, Paul, who was three years older, approached CHADD about working at the Miami Bureau of Investigation (MBI). Paul had just become a deputy sheriff and knew of openings within other agencies. Paul told CHADD that the MBI was perfect for him. CHADD had the background and the attitude that would fit a con-fidential informer (CI), especially after spending those years at Punta Cayenna. That offer sounded good to CHADD, and he met with Paul and discussed things with Paul's close friend Arnold, whom two other CIs report to.

Arnold asked CHADD to come by his office the next day, fill out the paperwork, and get ready for some training. CHADD left the meeting with Paul and Arnold and was looking forward to the next day.

CHADD walked into the sheriff's department and went to Arnold's office, filled out the paperwork, and got his schedule of the training sessions. Arnold knew of CHADD's past and told him that working with the MBI would be good for him—adventuresome and a way to release his anger while benefiting society. CHADD really didn't care about society at this point. He was definitely full of anger and rage and wanted to let it all out. He was doing this for himself, not for anyone else.

Arnold told him they would never meet at the department again after the first day. It would be too dangerous. If anyone knew he worked for the MBI, his life would be in danger. Arnold gave him a few little cases to work on. Infiltrate a gang who specialized in petty crimes, another in home invasion stealing TVs and jewelry, and another in stealing vehicles.

CHADD did rather well during this time at the MBI. He worked with Arnold, would see Paul regularly, and lived at home with his father and stepmother. He enjoyed his work; it was like he was getting even with the people that had made his life miserable. He had a great satisfaction from it all.

He had worked for two years with the MBI before Arnold gave him a big case. Arnold gave him the details and assigned him a hand-gun for protection. Arnold also knew that any drug dealer would have a weapon and wanted CHADD to fit the part. Arnold assigned him to work the case with a CI named Hector, who was already working on the inside with the gang.

Hector met CHADD in May during the Cuban festival in the Latin Quarter at Numero Uno, a restaurant in the middle of the Latin Quarter. They knew what each other looked like. They met there so people would get used to seeing them together. They hung out for a couple of weeks until the day came where Hector took him to meet the rest of the gang.

Hector took CHADD to a condo on the beach. Hector told him that everyone was extremely dangerous and to be careful all the time and don't trust any of them. They pulled into the parking lot and parked the car. They took the elevator to the third floor to room 3013. Hector rang the doorbell and the door was opened. Four guys in plain sight immediately reached for their weapons when they saw CHADD. No one had heard anything about him or met him before. Then everyone heard a voice speak out, "Don't worry about him. He is an old friend."

From around the corner, walking out from the kitchen came Marco. CHADD had not seen or heard from him since he left Serenity Bay a year before CHADD. Marco didn't change for the good. By being in Serenity Bay, he learned to be even more of a thief and manipulator. Everyone sat down in the living room looking over the ocean. He told everyone that if it were not for CHADD maintaining his silence for six months, he would have been severely punished. He left the island a month before CHADD and was taken off OP and only with CHADD's help did he escape the horrors of Punta Cayenna. He told everyone that he owed his life to CHADD and not to worry about him. Marco told the gang that he never knew CHADD to rat out anyone at Punta Cayenna no matter how much pain he had to endure to keep the trust of his fellow inmates.

CHADD was finding everything quite confusing now. Seeing Marco again brought back the misery and memories that he lived for four years. His hatred for his father surfaced again. He felt like he did while doing time on the island and in Alabama.

Marco took CHADD outside on the patio. Marco was always a bragger and wanted to impress CHADD on how big he had become. Marco told him about the big operation he had going on. He told CHADD that he would take cash into the federal building in Miami, buy drugs, drive them to his cousin in the Bronx, get more cash, and then buy more drugs. The cycle would continue week after week. CHADD asked Marco if he really bought the drugs at the federal building. He said no doubt about it. CHADD asked why the government was involved.

Marco said he didn't know and really didn't care. He had been working that routine for two years and made a lot of money. He said it was a piece of cake because he was protected driving up to New York because an unmarked government car and two agents escorted him. Any time they had been stopped for speeding or a rival gang tried to lift the drugs, the agents would spring into action on Marco's behalf. He loved the setup.

Marco never shared this information with anyone else. Only with his cousin and his contact at the federal building knew. Hector and CHADD left after a few hours of watching the Miami Dolphins play on TV. CHADD was asked what he and Marco spoke about and CHADD told Hector just making small talk, nothing important.

CHADD started having flashbacks of his days of Punta Cayenna. All the pain he endured for many years, he wanted his father and stepmother to pay.

After a few months of being one of the gang, Marco and CHADD went to the Numero Uno for dinner. Marco was leaving on his trip to the Bronx in a couple of days, so they wanted to spend some time at South Beach cruising the clubs. While sitting at the table, CHADD dropped his phone accidentally. He picked it up and put it on the table. When doing so, his black medallion came out from around his neck to the front of his shirt. He started to tuck it back in.

Marco said, "Whoa, whoa, brother. What is that? Where did you get that? I've never seen you wear it before. The dude at the federal building wears one just like that!" CHADD knew that there were only two in this world.

CHADD asked more about the guy. "What is his name? What does he look like?"

Marco told him, "His name is Mr. E," and described CHADD's father to the T.

Marco and CHADD continued their night on the town, but the entire night CHADD, was planning on how he was going to use the information and how he was going to make his father pay for what he had done to him.

Getting Even

CHADD had dreamed of an opportunity like this. He pondered and plotted on what he was going to do. What would hurt his father the most? What would make him pay for the years he had taken from his childhood—years that he could never get back—and the pain he caused his mother? This would not go unpunished.

Labor Day was coming up, and CHADD knew his father and his wife would be going out of town for a long weekend. He was going to be alone in the house. He waited for the time to strike. He was patient. His father's study was always locked, but CHADD had learned much at Punta Cayenna; not everything was on the brainwashing audio tapes that he was forced to listen to every day and night. for four years. He picked the lock and turned on his father's computer.

Part of CHADD's training by the MBI was hacking into computers. It took CHADD a couple of hours, and he started to look at emails to Mr. Jones while he was in the ICHANGE center in Punta Cayenna. These emails were concerning his mother and how Mr. Jones was directed to keep him in the center until his father contacted him. Mr. Jones told his father that he was going to win the case because people at the agency had already determined it. Edward would contact Mr. Jones a week ahead of time to let him know when to have CHADD ready.

CHADD also found other emails that made him angry. Emails about putting him in OP to see how long it would take to break him. Changing his medication without telling him and telling him his mother didn't love him or want to see him. All things to control and influence CHADD to gravitate to his father and away from his mother. He now knew the truth about his life at Punta Cayenna.

The most startling information he found was about what he was doing with Marco. Not only emails but documents too. CHADD found out all about the operation; the funds given to his father were actually used to purchase untraceable weapons for a special division of the NSA called the Guardians—a group that operated under the radar, not seen by Congress, and buried within the government. No funds were given to the Guardians, whom were receiving the drugs for sale by the agreements in place with the NSA, CIA, ATF, and border patrol. It was a perfect setup for everyone: steal the drugs from drug traffickers and resell them for cash. Protect a small group that could be trusted and keep the cycle going. Weapons could be purchased on the black market and flown in CIA planes without question.

CHADD downloaded all of the e-mails and documents onto a memory stick and left the house. He waited until his father returned the following Tuesday for their big talk.

CHADD had moved out of his father's house and was staying with Hector. He knew that once he had his conversation with his father, he was not going back to the house. CHADD had asked his father to meet him at a public place. They often spent time at the mall, and that seemed the perfect place to meet him.

His dad approached him on the bench in front of the computer store. CHADD began the conversation by telling him he remembered all of the terrible things that he had been through.

He also knew all about his operation with Marco. He wanted big cash to keep his mouth shut and not go to the papers. He also told his father everything he knew would be sent to the *Miami Herald* if he did not buy him a new car and put a million dollars in an offshore account. CHADD told his dad it was nothing personal, just payback for what he did to his mom and him.

Edward was in shock. He had no idea how CHADD found out all of the information. He told CHADD he would have to talk to the agency and advise them of his demands. CHADD told his dad that he knew the drug deals were often worth over a million dollars and the agency could handle him. It was a small price to pay for his silence. Edward had never seen CHADD this vengeful before and asked for forty-eight hours to get him the money.

CHADD responded, "I'll be fair. I'll give you twenty-four hours. The clock is ticking. And just to let you know, if anything happens to me, all of the information will be sent to the papers and CNN. Don't be stupid and mess with me."

Edward knew agency procedures. When under attack, always advise the agency immediately and let them decide. The two then went their separate ways and CHADD feeling a big payday was coming. His dad walked away knowing the meeting could be the last time he ever saw his son alive.

Edward got in his car and called Katherine and asked her to meet him away from the house. They met at the dock near their house. Katherine was furious and knew this could get out of hand and heads could roll. Edward didn't know if the house was bugged and needed to be away from there that's why they met at the dock. They were both very paranoid and called their contact at the agency and asked if he could meet him at their office at the federal building. He agreed and they drove to Miami and hustled into the building.

Lightning, Thunder, and Hail at the Clock Tower Center

I had gone to the coffee shop to meet CHADD and waited for a few hours, but he did not show up. I called Ethel and told her what happened. She called CHADD and then called me back. She told me that CHADD had to go with Katherine to meet some of her family.

Ethel then saw CHADD on the following Monday and called me. I asked her to let me speak to him. We agreed to meet the next morning for coffee. This is where the channeling and the spiritual awakening started happening for both of us.

I decided to talk to him as we took a drive. We "rode the lightning," where God spoke very loud and clear. It has not stopped since. We were told to listen to a CD called *Riding the Lightning*. Then we were instructed to get to a specific place and a designated parking place. We were safe under a tree and close to a clock when the thun-der and hail was falling in the size of golf balls everywhere around us. We were never touched, but the clock tower was struck by lightning and stopped the clock. He told me how his sixth sense had the chan-nel open to it through his experiences in the hospitals.

He only had flashbacks, but he knew he was more sensitive after his near-death experience.

We knew that we had a mission from God together. We decided to work together after I had given him training with Light and Sound therapies.

He had a great time and went back home very excited and told his stepmom. We got together again after ten days, and I began to work on him at my office with light, essential oils, and sound therapy to help his physical and spiritual bodies. We met several times a week for a month, and he told me that he was really feeling better. When we would meet, we spoke during the session, but he would leave almost immediately and return home. CHADD told me his stepmom always wanted to know where he was at all times. He also told me that he was considering having surgery on his feet because he wanted to walk again.

CHADD is was adjusting living in the real world every day, and I found it difficult at times to believe some of the stories he had been telling me.

After a month of spending time with me and talking about the metaphysical world and what God had been telling him, he went home and told his stepmom about wanting to have the surgery. A couple of days later, she told him that she had made an appointment in Gainesville to see a surgeon: to do the operation. They drove to Tampa and had lunch. Then they went to the hospital supposedly to meet the surgeon.

When they arrived at the hospital, his stepmother helped him into the wheelchair and pushed him into the hospital where two orderlies were waiting. She gave CHADD to them and he had a beleaguered look on his face. One of the nurses walked over to CHADD and took CHADD into her arms. She was a big woman and well-endowed and pushed his face into her chest and said, "Smile!" CHADD saw a flash and realized someone had taken a pic-ture of him with this nurse.

CHADD was moved into a private room as he began question-ing what was going on. He had thought he was there for the surgery to help him walk again. He was placed on the bed by the two order lies. They did not leave the room. After about an hour, the doctor came into the room. CHADD spoke about his surgery, but the doctor began speaking out his behavior. The doctor told CHADD that his stepmother had told him about his change in his behavior that was very concerning to her. That CHADD was not listening to her, that he was hearing voices and speaking to God, and was more defiant and rebellious. The doctor told CHADD he was staying there for observation and treatments. The orderlies had moved closer to CHADD in the event he tried to resist—which he did. They held him in place while the doctor gave him an injection. CHADD was screaming for help, but no one was there to help.

CHADD was moved to the mental ward once he was sedated. When he awakened, he found the world that had become very familiar to him. He was tied to his bed naked, had an orderly outside his door, and was monitored every hour by a nurse. He would be visited by a doctor that asked him some very strange questions about what he was hearing and seeing. The doctor kept telling him that he was delusional and was trying to discredit his visions and his clairaudience abilities.

After three days of being forced to be injected with medication, CHADD had to use the bathroom. By this time, he had been moved to another room that was more like a cell. The orderly entered his room and released him from his restraints. He staggered to the bathroom nude. He sat on the toilet and fell unconscious. When he awakened, he had two black eyes and a welt on the side of his head. The orderly that was in charge of watching him told him if he did anything else that reflected bad on him, that he would beat him so bad, the fall he just had would be nothing in comparison. For the next three days of his stay in the hospital, he was afraid for his life and he would fight to stay alive.

This stay at the hospital, once again, was not good for CHADD. The doctor kept giving him overdoses of drugs with terrible side effects at such a point that he could not speak anymore, neither was he able to transfer himself from his wheelchair. He screamed for twenty minutes before the orderly came and helped him when he fell off of the toilet. He was naked and in a fetal position and had dark circles under his eyes. During the time on the toilette, a camera was watching the entire scenario. His tongue was out of his mouth only a few inches from the urine on the floor.

I called CHADD's mom everyday while he was gone. I didn't know what happened to him. The only things known to Ethel was what Edward told her. Edward said CHADD had been hospitalized because of his erratic behavior caused by his misuse of drugs. I certainly never saw that during our therapy sessions together in the proceeding month. When I saw him, after this last stay at the hospital, he looked anemic, malnourished, and his skin was grey. He did not know how to interact with anyone or sustain direct eye contact. He would always wear dark sunglasses. His eyes were very sensitive to light, and he could hardly see. He was horribly dressed, but you could tell he had a certain class and intelligence underneath his distressing appearance.

He was labeled with various diagnoses over the years for ADD, brain damage, borderline personality disorder, and bipolar. Most of the drugs were addictive and had their own side effects. He had just started showing epileptic symptoms and an irregular heartbeat. A week after leaving the hospital, he showed signs of a bleeding ulcer. He was now totally unable to live and function normally.

Over the next month, he asked the doctor to lower his dosage of what he was on at any given time, and the MD doubled the dosage instead.

After a month of seeing his deterioration when he was with his mom, I decided to have a meeting with his stepmom. I met her at the Java Bean Bistro for coffee and asked her to come by my office for a Light and Sound session. I hoped that by her experiencing the therapy, she would see that I was not a threat to CHADD and would allow me access to him to continue our relationship. I was in the process of using the light, and I glanced into the mirror at her face. I saw her face as distorted and not what I saw when I looked at her directly. I knew something was strange about her because the light was acting erratically when it would hit her body. She was a dark energy and was different from everyone I had treated before. I know CHADD was surrounded by energy that would ultimately destroy him if I didn't find a way to get closer to him.

Three months had passed, and I had started seeing CHADD again. It wasn't very often, but at least his stepmom didn't seem to see me as a threat to her or CHADD. I started to bring him back to health by treating him with the Light and Sound. I researched his drugs and told him what I found. He had become addicted to the drugs he was taking, but he was trying to get off of them. He, at times, seemed closer to normal but still had moments of irritability and confusion.

CHADD's stepmother bought him an iPhone so she could keep in contact with him if she ever wanted to talk to him. He loved the phone. It was the first real electronic toy that he had since he was twelve.

I had first met CHADD in April, and now it was late May. This is when I experienced the breath of God. Since the first day we met, we have been totally guided by our spiritual family to do some specific spiritual work. In May, I drove us to visit a park not far from his home. This park was very familiar and peaceful for him. We sat under a tree next to a bush not far from a lake. A strong breeze came from nowhere and took us by surprise. CHADD was looking at me, smiling, as we both were experiencing the power and beauty of God's breath. That power and beauty allowed us to touch into a vortex at higher spiritual levels. Around the vortex was complete stillness, and we could observe the leaves that were falling from the trees but were caught up in the spirals and lifted up toward the sky. The vortex allowed us to be enlightened with clarity and connectivity with the divine. I had never experienced such a thing before. I heard the name Foue shortly after we had experienced the vortex.

I introduced CHADD to the spirit of a tree that I thought I heard the name Foue. I told him that he could speak to the spirit of the tree. CHADD put his hand on the tree and heard a voice saying, "My name is Frey instead of Foue." CHADD thanked the spirit for that information. His palm's print left a mark of energy on the tree that lasted for three days.

I asked the spirit to come out of the tree and stand next to us. That caught CHADD totally by surprise. Then CHADD said, "What is that?" I explained that it was the spirit of the tree that was called out to be with us. Then Frey told us that he wanted to spend the day with us. We left the park in late morning on our way to com-plete our tasks for the day.

Frey joined us until dusk. It was quite a day with a spirit. We drove to the local café for lunch. CHADD and I were speaking tele-pathically to Frey, and we were all enjoying the knowledge and com-panionship of the day. We left lunch and went to the office. Frey spent the time with us as we had sessions on clients. After our work for the day was over, we drove back to the park with Frey. CHADD went back to the tree and put his hand back at the same location that he had put his hand earlier. It was a very enjoyable day for all three of us. The following night, Frey gave to CHADD a dream with a song to interpret that was full of humor.

Summer of Chaos

During this summer of chaos and after a long day of work-ing at a metaphysical level with CHADD, we both were hungry and decided to go get something to eat. We drove to the Red Rock restaurant, and after we were seated, we ordered something to drink and eat. We drank some alcoholic beverages and talked about our day together. After we ate our meal, we asked the server for our check. We waited for a long time for our server to come back with our check, so we decided to go to the reception desk to pay for our dinner. As I was pushing CHADD's wheelchair, I could feel I was going into an out-of-body experience, and in what seemed like seconds, I could feel myself coming back into my body. My wrists hurt and I looked down and saw that I had handcuffs on. I looked over to CHADD and he was on the ground, and the officers roughly picked him up and pulled him with his feet dragging behind him, and he was pushed into a sheriff's car. They pushed me toward the car on the other side of CHADD and ordered me to get into the car. It was very uncomfortable sitting in the car with my hands in hand-cuffs behind my back—still not knowing what had happened and why I was being taken to the station.

When we got to the station, they picked up CHADD and dropped him on his head before they put him in his wheelchair and escorted us both into the station. When we got inside, they ushered CHADD into a separate room, and they took off his shoes and shirt. The officer told me to go over to the computer in the cubicle so they could process me. I was still in shock and did not understand what had happened. The lady behind the computer was ignoring me as I stood there. She did not even look up at me or say anything while I was standing there. I heard someone on the other side of the cubicle groaning and moaning like they were in pain. I wondered who it was and why they were in pain. Finally, the lady asked me some questions then asked me to remove all my jewelry and she also asked for my cell phone. Then I was ushered into another room that had one wall of windows and a metal bench with no blanket or restroom. I pleaded with the officer to let me call my son because I knew he was very worried about me. The officer told me to shut up and to wait, and I still was not told why I was there. The officers pushed my face against the glass with my arms and legs stretched out. I noticed some flashes and realized they were taking pictures of me.

When the officer left, I looked out of the window and saw that it was a hallway. I could see people further down the hall and wondered where CHADD was. I knew that he had been there for a very long time but did not know what time it was. I was astonished to see I had bruises forming on both of my arms, from my wrists down to my elbows. Since I had no recollection of how they got there, I believe the bruising was caused when they put the handcuffs on me. I was lying down on the metal bench, facing away from the windows, waiting for the officer to return so I could make my phone call.

In the morning, when the officer came, she brought me breakfast. I told her that I was not hungry and was not going to eat food from the jailhouse. I asked again if I could call my family, and she told me there would be no phone calls yet. I told her I have the right to call my lawyer. The officer told me to shut up and that I would get my chance later to make a phone call. I was taken to a room where I was told to strip down and to put my cloths into one bag and the clothes from the jail into another bag and put them down a chute. I was told to take a shower. I told her that I was not going to take a shower there, and I did not want to put on the cloths that were given to me to wear. I stood there naked, waiting for something to wear and waiting for someone to tell me why I was there. The room was all glass and I could see people looking at me. I was not going to let them see me embarrassed, so I gave them the peace sign and smiled. I decided to take a shower, hoping it would get me out of there faster. They took me to another room, and I was given a jumpsuit to put on and waited.

When the officer returned, I could see it was a different officer and was told it was a shift change. The officer seemed to be nicer than the other officers I dealt with, and I could hear him talk to other officers and realized he was French. I followed him and he stopped and looked down and saw that I only had one shoe on and asked me to put on my other shoe. I asked the new officer if I could make my phone call and was finally granted my wish. My family was very worried about me since I did not return home the night before. They had called the hospitals, friends, and also the police station but did not find my whereabouts.

The officer handed me some paperwork. The paperwork stated, "Arguing and fighting with security. Did not pay the check before leaving establishment."

I looked up at the officer and said, "Is this a joke?"

The officer said no. He explained that I was arrested because I was hitting the security guard at the restaurant.

I said, "Surely this is a joke."

He looked at me, shook his head, and said, "Yes it is."

To which I replied, "If it is a joke, it is not a very funny one." Then the officer threw the paperwork in front of me and told me I needed to sign the paperwork so I could be released. I signed the paperwork so I could get out of there. I needed to go back with the money so I could get CHADD released also. They gave me my jewelry, and I looked through it and did not see my cell phone or my Vajra. I asked the officer where they were, and he said they were not in my personal belongings and then produced a picture with my jewelry and in the picture my cell phone and Vajra was not there. I questioned him about it and he told me that whoever processed me is responsible for taking the pictures of all prisoners' belongings. I told him whoever knows me knows that I do not go anywhere without my Vajra.

They gave me paperwork that was folded up and I left. As I was leaving, one of the female officers looked at me and yelled, "Get out of here and never come back! If I ever see you here again, I'll beat the shit out of you." She then disappeared behind a door.

I could not wait to get home to take a shower and get some rest. It was not comfortable sleeping on the metal bench, and I was exhausted from everything that had happened to me in the last twen-ty-four hours. When I got home, I took a shower, ate, and fell to sleep. I woke up the next day, and I realized I did not have my car; it was still at Red Rock. I drove down to the restaurant, went up to the reception desk, and asked for my keys. As soon as they saw me, they called security and I was ushered outside. Police cars had arrived as soon as I walked out of the door of the restaurant. Again, I would be taken into custody. I showed no resistance and asked them not to put the handcuffs on too tight. Off to the station I went.

I did not realize that Red Rock had filed a restraining order on me, and I was not allowed within one hundred feet of the establishment. I explained to them that my car was at the restaurant, and I needed to pick it up. My family arrived to take me home, but first I wanted to bail out CHADD. We processed the paperwork and CHADD's mother came to take him home.

My family took me home. They told me that they would go Red Rock and pick up the car. When my family arrived at the restau-rant, they went to the reception area and asked to see the manager. When the manager arrived, he greeted them. My family explained to the manager that they wanted to pay my check and pick up my car. The manager handed my family the check, and they used my credit card to pay the bill and also gave 20 percent gratuity to the server.

All Fell into Place

My experiences with CHADD, family conflict, time in jail, monitoring by the government, and many other situations gave me pause to start doubting myself, my mission, and God. However, I knew I had to continue, so I asked during a meditation what all of this meant. Things have gotten worse, people have died, and I had more questions than answers.

CHADD was in a mental facility again under constant physical and spiritual attacks, and I could not help him. I contacted a friend, Pierre, at the Louvre, who understood ancient societies, legends, and artifacts. I met him on one of my many visits to the museum when I was a flight attendant during a layover. I reached out to him, hoping he could help me resolve some things that I have noticed and what I been through.

Fortunately, Pierre was available to see me whenever I arrived. I knew that I was under constant surveillance and being monitored, so I did not give him too much information of what I wanted to discuss. With Homeland Security policies in place, I knew it was not safe, in any way, to inform him of anything until we were able to meet. I booked a flight from the Miami International Airport via Air France and flew to Paris and landed at Charles de Gaulle Airport.

During my ten-hour flight, I thought about my time with CHADD over and over in my mind. I wrote down everything that I could remember because I knew I would only get one chance to speak with Pierre on this trip.

I remembered my first meeting with Edward and when I saw his medallion. I also remember listening to Henri's story and the medallion that CHADD was wearing when I first met him. How could one medallion be found in the Rockies in the 1800s and the other a gift from the ancient city of Antioch? Did any of it fit together, or was it just another of those strange coincidences that we often see in the world?

Reading Henri's memoirs, I noticed a reference to a little known Christian sect that saw a definite battle of love and materialism in the world of their day. Something that has gotten even more defined. That group was known as Cathari throughout history, its roots in Jerusalem soon after Christ was crucified.

When I landed at the airport, I immediately went to the Louvre. Pierre was waiting for me and greeted me with enthusiasm. Soon I was going to find out things that I had no idea was possible.

The enlightenment from Pierre started flowing from him. He said that the Cathari had traveled from Jerusalem and took advantage of the religious freedom for Christianity that were found in the City of God in AD 300. They built the Great Church and were the pri-mary Christian group in the City of God for almost three hundred years.

The Cathari realized the end of their days were quickly approaching since the Persians were continuously sacking the city. So they took most of their holy items and headed north through Turkey continuing to Northern Italy. This was not a good place for them to stay because they were considered heretics by the Roman Catholic Church.

The Cathari believed in a God of good and a God of evil. The Cathari did not believe in one all-encompassing God, but in two, both equal and comparable in status. They believed that the physical world was evil and was created to encompass all that was corporeal, chaotic, and powerful. The God of good was entirely disincarnate: a being of pure spirit and completely unsullied by the taint of matter. He was the God of love, order, and peace.

Love and power were completely incompatible, and matter was seen as a manifestation of power, which also was incompatible with love.

The Cathari had two general categories, the Perfecti (Perfects) and the Credentes (Believers). The Perfecti formed the core of the religion. The Perfecti represented the heart of the Cathari tradition, the true Christian Church, as they believed themselves to be. The new Perfectus surrendered his or her worldly goods to the commu-nity and the Credentes. The Perfectus undertook a life dedicated to following the example of Christ and his apostles. Attempting to devote one's life to purity, prayer, preaching, and doing charitable work. Above all, they were dedicated to enabling others to find the road that led from the dark land ruled by the dark lord. In all of my research, I could not find where exactly the dark land was and who was the dark lord; Pierre did.

His name was Rex Mundi, and I recognized the name imme-diately when I heard it. The same last name as the president of the United States and owner of ICHANGE, which owned the behavior center that had imprisoned CHADD in the center at Punta Cayenna. I couldn't believe it.

Pierre continued to tell me that the Cathari believed that Jesus had been a manifestation of spirit unbounded by the limitation of matter, a sort of Divine spirit or feelings manifesting within human beings. They proclaimed that the God of the Old Testament was really the devil, or creative demiurge. They also believed that there was a higher god—the true god—and Jesus was described as being that True God, or his messenger.

Besides the New Testament, the three sacred texts to the Cathari were *The Gospel of the Secret Supper* (or *John's Interrogation*), *The Book of the Two Principles*, and the *Book of Enoch*.

The God found in the Old Testament had nothing to do with love known to the Cathari. The Old Testament God had created the world as a prison and demanded from the "prisoners" fearful obedi-ence and worship. This God was the God worshiped by the Roman Catholics, the God that tormented and murdered "his children."

They also abstained from all animal food and refused to kill, even in war. They were also considered Buddhists because of their belief that the doctrine of resurrection taught by Jesus was similar to the Buddhist doctrine of rebirth or reincarnation. All of these things continually were against the Roman Catholic Church and their teachings.

The Cathari had moved into France because of the constant persecution in Italy. Pope Eugene III began a policy to stop the progress of the Cathari in 1147. It culminated in the massacre on July 22, 1209. The doors of Saint Mary Magdalene were broken down and the refugees dragged out and slaughtered, supposedly seven thousand people died there. Elsewhere in the town, many more thousands were mutilated and killed. Prisoners were blinded, dragged behind horses, and used for target practice. What remained of the city was razed by fire. The leader of crusaders wrote, "Today, Your Holiness, 20,000 heretics were put to the sword, regardless of rank, age or sex." When asked how would his soldiers tell the difference from Cathari and Catholics, he replied, "Kill them all, the Lord will recognize His own."

A popular unsubstantiated theory holds that a small party of Cathari escaped from the town before the massacre. It is widely believed that the escapees took with them a treasure.

What this treasure consisted of has been a matter of consid-erable speculation. Claims range from sacred texts to accumulated wealth, and even the Holy Grail. Then they scattered into the forests and mountains and eventually disappeared with occasional references throughout the centuries on several continents of their existence.

Protestant and Jehovah's Witness theology both share beliefs held by the Cathari. I wondered, *How did that happen?* I thought, *How can two medallions be found in two completely parts of the world and share so many things in common? Did the Cathari survive the mas-sacre and reach America with their treasure? What was the mysterious writing on the medallions, and how old were they and why did they have the* Book of Enoch *as one of their sacred texts?* These pieces of the puz-zle were not answering questions but creating them.

Pierre had studied the Middle East and Persian Empire for decades, and he was filling in the blanks so I continued to ask him more.

Here is where my spiritual beliefs helped piece everything together. Pierre began by telling me that there is very little difference between truth, myths, and legends when it came to God. His knowl-edge also came from the Dead Sea Scrolls, the Bible, and the missing books of the Bible.

I never expected to hear his amazing details that would fill in the blanks of my path with CHADD. He started answering my questions one by one and was enjoying it. He said that ancient writings stated that a comet, in the form of a black boulder created before time began, sent a fragment of heaven to earth. It was found by the ancient Hebrews, and the story was found in the hieroglyphics inside the Temple of Seti in Egypt. The Hebrews then broke apart the boulder and shaped the boulder into two medallions—one showing a flame and the other of water. Each had Hebrew inscriptions on them. The legend spoke of angels of God creating the medallions and speaking to the Hebrew masons to put a message on each one. The oldest recorded language was considered over five thousand years old, strangely the oldest writing told a story of God sending his angels to save the earth. The medallions were then moved to the Temple of Solomon on Mount Moriah. Just before the Temple of Solomon was destroyed, the medallions were moved to Jerusalem, where they stayed until Jesus died. For centuries, they disappeared until a legend spoke of the medallions surfacing with a Christian group that faded into time. The group was the Cathari in the third-century BC. They are the descendants of the two hundred fallen angels of heaven that came down to earth to mate with human females. That is where the duality began, angels of great beauty and light while at the same time turning against the world of God. Twice this event happened, the first time before the Great Flood and again after the Great Flood. Hebrews were commanded to seek and destroy all humans that were created out of those unclean unions; however, not all were destroyed.

That is where the truth gets blurry, some stories tell of the warring factions of the Cathari—those of spirit and those of the material world, the fight between good and evil. It is believed these two elements have existed since the beginning of time.

The Perfecti and Credentes separated paths but continually were at odds with one another. The Perfecti believed that they were the only ones that could stop and control the Credentes. The Perfecti had members such as Abraham Lincoln, George Washington, Gandhi, and Mother Teresa. The Credentes were the materialistic and greedy, such as Hitler, Attila the Hun, and Genghis Khan. They gained material things in this world by destroying anyone or any-thing that stood in their way.

The Perfecti were told to have taken a great treasure with them as they passed through the British Isles. Staying for a time in Scotland, their presence can be seen in the mounds that are found in Scotland and America. They moved to America passing through Nova Scotia and leaving clues to the Ark of the Covenant. The two factions became transparent in almost every country of the world, with one polarity offsetting the other and always trying to gain control.

I had taken photos of CHADD's medallion and told Pierre of Edward's, so I transferred the photo from my memory stick to his office computer so he could study it. He was in total amazement, and he told me that he did not recognize the writing, that it was definitely a form of Hebrew, but not entirely. It was a combination of different languages. His face lit up and acted like he just won the lottery. I told him the medallion was found by Henri and had been worn by the Indian Jesus in the 1800s, and his face almost turned white as a sheet. Pierre said all of this had been prophesied in the Dead Sea Scrolls as well as by Nostradamus, Edgar Cayce, and other sensitives. When heaven and earth reunite, there will be a new beginning, a new world order.

I spent the whole day with Pierre. He was extremely knowledge-able and even took me to see the mosaics that Henri had uncovered in Antioch that were on display there. One of the mosaics showed two groups and had flowing water and a part of the town was burn-ing. I decided it was time to come home.

Pierre told me he felt uncomfortable telling me another leg-end that had to do with the *Book of Enoch* and the Cathari. He said that the descendants of the angels and earth females were said to be slightly deformed because of the new sequence of DNA components. The fathers were definitely not from earth; they knew about cloning and combining DNA from humans and other creatures. In cultures throughout time, they were known as werewolves, reptilians, Bigfoots, vampires, and other unknown and unique creatures that were all genetically altered.

Pierre told me this was the most interesting day of his career. He wished me well and told me that he would contact me when he researched the medallion. I told him it may not be safe to be in contact with me. I knew during this time of terrorists, every e-mail and phone conversation was monitored. I even had to leave my phone at home. I advised him that I would contact him by either writing, in person, by messenger, or by a secure Internet connection.

He understood and I thanked him and went to my hotel across the river near Notre Dame. I left a day later, digesting and trying to remember everything that had happened with CHADD.

Revealed

few days later, we went to the hotel in the Sunshine State Mall for a metaphysical convention, and we were demon-strating Light and Sound healing, an alternative form of medicine. We sensed strange energies around us before the conven-tion. It was our first public appearance together as the God Duo. We had achieved a 2000 percent profit that day, and we were politely asked not to come back the next day. The convention promoter gave me a refund for the entire time of the show and was not given an explanation as to why. I was then offered a sizable amount of money to keep my silence involving the activities surrounding my removal from the convention. I believe it was because of the difference in faith between the promoters and myself.

CHADD was telling me during the day that he felt we were being watched. He noticed four men, in groups of two, that were standing from a distance watching us. CHADD said that they all looked like the soldier that had been at the hospital when his father Edward first had him admitted and drugged. He doubted his mem-ory because all he had been through after Punta Cayenna. He, at first, thought it was just his imagination playing tricks on him, but after he thought about it, he believed that memory fragments were being released in his subconscious mind and coming to the surface. We also noticed there were several unknown men taking photos of us. I picked up a strong psychic message from one of the four men. It was a very unusual message, but God was protecting us and I knew noth-ing bad would happen to us. Having psychic abilities since my youth, I knew some messages could be jumbled and sometimes would come in images, voices, and other spiritual connections. I tried to receive more information, but it seemed the path to this person was being blocked. For twenty minutes, I was receiving conflicting messages and was very confused.

A woman requested a session with me. While I was giving her Light and Sound therapy, I looked into her eyes and I could read her intentions. Her main intent was to challenge me and verify that I had the knowledge of the effects created by Light and Sound on a person and if I had connection to the force. She wanted to experience the effect herself. After the session, she grabbed me and cried, then quickly composed herself because she knew others were observing her in her group.

It was late July when CHADD had gotten his driver's license. He picked me up in the "holy running car" and said, "We are going on a spiritual mission again today." We were guided that day to go to Siesta Key and stopped on our way to get a cup of coffee. We ended up under a gigantic, majestic, and splendid banyan that had existed for many years.

Facing us on the door of the building next to it was written "U2." The day was beginning very well, and we were guided to go between the buildings facing the water. We were amazed by the spec-tacular display in front of us. There were various kinds of fish, vary-ing in size, flying and performing acrobatics in the water for us. We stayed there observing the water and the show for a long time. We were in perfect harmony with nature, the water, and the fish. We were outside of time in another dimension, receiving all kind of spiritual messages, information, signs, and warnings that day. CHADD and I met at the office the day after we got back from Siesta Key, and I gave him another therapy session. His stepmother found out about the convention and told him he was spending too much time with me and was concerned that I was influencing him to rebel against her. CHADD was very afraid of both his father and stepmother, so we decided to let things cool off for a few weeks. CHADD had missed out on his childhood, so he wanted to go and stay at a hotel on South Beach and spend time with other people his age. When CHADD called me, I told him we would meet the next afternoon.

My first impression and intuition for the day was not good. I was getting a bad vibe. The morning of our meeting, CHADD was awakened by a loud siren and the lights turned on. CHADD knew it was a fire alarm in the building and decided to ignore it and went to take his shower so he could leave soon. He had arranged to pick up his old friend and bring him back to the hotel. He called the front desk to ask for his car to be brought to the valet area. When he went outside the hotel, a taxi drove up to him and the valet refused to give CHADD his keys. The valet forced him to get inside the taxi and put his wheelchair in the trunk. As they drove away, CHADD was telling the driver that he did not have any cash to pay him and wanted him to stop and put him on the sidewalk. CHADD felt he was being kidnapped and started tapping on the driver's shoulder to make him stop. The driver pulled over to where a police car was parked.

The driver casually got out of the car and so did the police officer. They spoke to each other for a moment, and the driver nod-ded. It seemed like they knew each other. The police officer then used his radio, which was located on his shoulder, to call someone, but CHADD could not hear what was said. Suddenly an ambulance drove up and the attendants got out and grabbed CHADD and put him on a gurney. They strapped him in and wheeled him into the ambulance. CHADD began to scream and immediately he was given sedatives. They took him to a mental facility without ever asking him for his ID.

When I arrived at the hotel, I saw CHADD's SUV, but he was nowhere to be found. I asked the doorman if he had seen someone in a wheelchair, and he told me a young man had gotten into a taxi. I was in shock and I wondered where he was. I immediately called the police in fear that he had been taken against his will. When I went to the police department to file a report, the detective had told me that he had heard about a guy in a wheelchair that was violent and was taken to a hospital. After I found out what hospital he had been taken to, I drove to the facility, but was told I was not allowed to see him until he was released in ten days.

A few days after he was admitted, he met a woman by the name of Letica. She gave CHADD a pile of papers to sign and told him that they were papers for him to work as a lifeguard at South Beach. How could he be a lifeguard when he couldn't even walk? He was so medicated, he would have signed anything, but CHADD would find out later what those papers were for.

Letica told CHADD to call her when he got out and told him that she worked at the hospital, and if he ever was stopped for a speeding ticket to just mention her name since all the officer's knew who she was. Katherine came to pick him up and he called Letica from the car, and she invited both of them for lunch that day. After lunch, Letica asked Katherine and CHADD to follow her to a beach house.

When they arrived, Letica told CHADD, "This house is for you! A house on the beach and it is accessible for your wheelchair." Then she told him that he had a job as a lifeguard and she had made it happen.

CHADD felt it was strange because it seemed that Letica and Katherine knew each other, but he wasn't sure since he had just gotten out of the hospital.

Katherine and CHADD drove back to her house. After dinner, CHADD went outside and called me. He told me the story of his last ten days. CHADD told me that Letica was having a party for him the next day, at his new beach house, but I could not drive him. I told him I needed to see him, that I had business to take care of for a couple of days and I would call him when I returned.

CHADD and I met two days later at the coffee shop, and I asked him, "Do you understand what is going on? She is trying to buy you. Letica, or someone else through her, is trying to buy you." He realized immediately and said, "No one will buy me. I am a man of God." Then he erased her number from his phone and stopped answering her calls. He had told me that the day of the party, she wanted him to come over early. She had champagne and had invited several people to his housewarming party.

I told him, "Don't you see, what better way for people that are out to destroy you, to make friends with you."

A stoic look came upon his face. He knew exactly what I meant. He also told me Katherine and his father went with him and mingled with everyone for hours. It seemed very strange to him since they all acted like they were old friends.

I asked him to try and remember what everyone looked like for future reference since I was certain he would see some of these people again. CHADD told me that some of the people looked familiar. He instantly started to have flashbacks to his days in the center at Punta Cayenna. He recognized two men who looked like they were guards from the center. He saw a man who looked like a doctor from the first mental hospital he was taken to. I knew CHADD was still under terrible withdrawal from his years of prescription drugs before his reinsertion into the world by me. He did not have all of mental abilities harnessed and was easy prey to those who were looking to take advantage of him.

After a couple of weeks, CHADD began his limited driving again. His father had picked up his SUV from the hotel while he was in the facility. He began to come by my office for the Light and Sound therapy again and was progressing very well with daily sessions.

CHADD told Katherine that we were going into partnership together. He would be the front man that would show everyone how helpful the therapy is. Katherine was unusually cooperative, which made me feel quite uneasy. I usually follow my gut feelings, and I became even more cautious but decided to move forward.

There was a metaphysical convention a month later in Tucson that CHADD's father gave him approval to attend with me. We flew to Arizona from Miami International Airport with a stop in Dallas. We had our first contact with Jesus at the airport. We met Jesus three times during our trip, and we both could sense his presence with us.

Two mornings after we arrived, I heard a knock on my door, and when I opened it, CHADD was with a man dressed all in white. CHADD said, "VIE, I am bringing you Jesus." The man did not talk but just stared at me and then mysteriously disappeared by dematerializing. I heard him one more time at our hotel, when I was waiting for the taxi to pick us up and drive us to the ancient spiritual Indian sites outside of Tuscan. CHADD had not come down to the lobby yet, and I heard the voice say, "Where is the handicapped man in the wheelchair?" I looked around the lobby and saw CHADD just exit-ing the elevator and coming toward us. Jesus then said, "No, where is the other handicapped man?" I then knew he referred to a man that I saw earlier in a seat whose energy attracted me. He seemed special, but I did not approach him and realized then that I had been ignoring a message. I looked everywhere at the hotel, but I did not find him.

In the middle of the next night, I was awakened by the lights that were located on both sides of my bed. The door was closed, and I looked around the room and knew I was alone, but I could feel a presence in the room with me.

In the morning, as we were walking around the convention, we noticed that the Twenty-Fifth Congress of Illumination was taking place at the same time. We decided to take part of two seminars that day. The energy that day for us was wonderful!

After the seminars, CHADD went into the restroom. I could sense that he was out of his wheelchair, pressed against the wall, fac-ing the entrance by an invisible spirit. As I ran into the bathroom to reach him, he could feel the spirit release him. He said to me, "Whoa! You just blessed the room!" I helped him get back into his wheelchair, and we left the restroom together.

The next morning, right after dawn, I decided to go for a walk on the trail outside the hotel. On each side of the trail, there were drawings of three hearts in the sand that looked exactly alike. There was a small one, a medium one around the first, and the larg-est around the other two. I wondered who created these beautiful drawings.

As I sat on a bench only a few hundred yards from the resort, I saw a beautiful, tall, slim woman with a very sweet face that was drawing more of them in the sand. I got up and walked over to speak to her and found out that she was originally from Germany but now was living in Fort Lauderdale. She only lived a few miles from where I lived in Florida.

After some small talk, I asked her if I could watch her as she created more art in the sand and she said it was fine. As she began to draw several of them, she made amazing sounds that resonated with my energy. She finished up her creations and then walked over and hugged me, still humming the sounds. My heart was melting, and I could tell we had admiration for each other. She gave me an explanation of the drawings; it was of the Father, the Son, and Mother Mary.

During our stay in Arizona, we met with messengers of God, and messages were delivered and many other wonderful things happened.

Inside the convention, I saw two Avatars approaching CHADD. I walked over to tell them what I thought of them, but they vanished quickly to bother other people. Shortly after that, I was contacted via cell phone by an Avatar coach. I could feel his bad energy so I hung up. He called back for a second time and asked for a meeting "to exchange knowledge." Strangely enough, I noticed that his voice changed from a Latino accent to an American accent.

On the last day of the convention, we attended a reception early in the morning. We left CHADD's business cards and a copy of his résumé on the table where other people could leave their information for networking purposes. When we returned from lunch to the reception area to mingle with the other attendees, we noticed all of CHADD's cards and résumés were gone! All of the other résumés were still there. Either someone did not want other people to see them or people who were interested in CHADD took them. We didn't know but left more business cards and résumés when we left.

The evening before we were scheduled to return to Miami, we were sitting on the balcony of my room looking at the sunset. We both had the same experience simultaneously; we traveled out of this dimension and we saw Egypt, the Sphinx, and the Eagle. I did not want to leave Arizona, but I knew there was work to be done for mankind in Florida.

On our way back to Florida, we had an hour delay due to bad weather. When we arrived at the airport, we went to the indicated gate to catch our plane. We were surprised when we got to the gate because we did not see anyone there. Suddenly a man that was alone and seated in one of the seats stood up, but we could only see his back.

He shouted out to us to go to another gate that was at the other side of the airport. I pushed CHADD's wheelchair toward the elevator to take us to the tram to the new gate. It was difficult getting CHADD into the tram because the door opened and closed automatically and the wheels got caught in the rails. It was late and all I really wanted was to take a nap. I also knew CHADD, who had been sitting in his wheelchair for so long, was tired too. CHADD never complained though; he had a sense of humor and always kept his smile.

We finally arrived at the boarding desk at the gate, and we were processed and we moved to the waiting area. It was after 1:00 a.m., and we heard the announcement that all flight departures or arrivals had been cancelled until the next morning due to the bad weather.

After we had been waiting for about an hour, one of the crew members gave us a coupon for dinner and told us we needed to wait for a special shuttle for CHADD. We waited for another hour before the shuttle came for us, and then we had something to eat and went to the hotel that was attached to the airport. When we got to our rooms, the beds were not made, so I went down to the front desk to get sheets, blankets, and pillows to make the beds and then only one of the two elevators were working!

The following day we went back to the airport and we boarded the plane. We were delayed again because of some technical difficulties and had to change to another plane an hour later. We finally took off and I observed that one of the crew members looked somewhat abnormal. All of the attendants were very athletic-looking types, and the pilot looked different, though in a very good sense.

A few days later, my good friend Guy Van came to visit me. He brought his wife, Arlene, who was from Singapore, and their son, David. I had not seen them in a few years since I left the island. He had emailed me to inform me that they were coming with their son for fifteen days, and then David would stay for a year to study at Palm Beach Atlantic University. We were colleagues and very good friends while working for the same airline. He met his wife while traveling in Singapore. I introduced Guy Van to CHADD on a previous visit, and ever since they have been very good friends. CHADD and I drove Guy Van's family around town to see the sights.

As we drove around town, I looked to the back seat and started laughing. Guy Van was hanging onto his wife tightly by the waist, and the other hand was gripping the handle that was hanging from the top of the door. They looked very serious and pretended nothing was happening, and no one said a word. Later that day, Guy Van made a comment to me, "CHADD thinks he is Speedy Gonzales!"

Guy Van and his wife told me a wonderful story of something that happened to them. Guy Van was in search of his spiritual path. He is originally from Vietnam. One day he traveled back there to pray under one of the spiritual trees and then went to Jerusalem and finished with a visit to Lourdes in France. While there, a miracle happened and he saw the white light. When he came back to the island, he was baptized. Since then Guy Van and his wife meditate and pray for the world several hours every week. Guy Van is now guided by the spirit of his grandfather that had crossed over.

Over the weekend, we traveled to visit a couple, John and Beth, who came from New Caledonia but then moved to Tampa Bay. We went to their house with their little two-year-old daughter, Emmanuelle, who was a gifted beauty with a very strong personality for such a young girl. CHADD was wearing his medallion, as he always did, and I wore my famous energy Vajra, which was based on a Sacred Geometric form and that also looks like a cross.

At first the little girl was very shy, but after a few minutes, she came right over to me and looked at the pendant. Then she gently took it between her little hands and brought it to her mouth to kiss it. After she did that, she went over to CHADD and did exactly the same thing to his medallion. The emotion was so strong that CHADD was not able to hide his tears behind his dark sunglasses. It was hard to believe what she knew at such a young age!

We left and drove the long drive home. CHADD and I both felt we were being followed and monitored. We had felt this way for months, but the feelings were now getting stronger. I didn't know if it was because of David or the new people in Tampa Bay we had brought into our circle.

CHADD told me that he felt that there were certain government agents involved. His stepbrother, Paul, had told him that the sheriff's department can monitor a person's whereabouts by following a person's cell phone tower usage. CHADD knew he was always under surveillance to some degree and felt that I was under the same daily occurrence. It seemed wherever I went, I could see or feel someone watching me. I knew I was not paranoid but had psychic abilities and was in tune with the energies surrounding me.

One evening the following weekend, CHADD went to the Douglas Auditorium to see a movie on South Africa but realized later that it was another setup. A man by the name of Mickael introduced himself and paid for CHADD's drink. He had a friend who suddenly showed up with a drink and then vanished. Then Mickael's ex-girlfriend joined him and CHADD. It seemed that both of them were quite popular in the area because photographers surrounded the three of them. After a few minutes, she left, saying to Mickael, "I've got to go. I've got to go."

CHADD was still trying to stay balanced and was experiencing terrible withdrawal symptoms from his prescription drugs. He was also having difficulty adjusting to the world after his first stay in the hospital, when he returned from the center in Punta Cayenna. Everything was still so new to him, after such a long time in seclusion at his father's house. CHADD was still easy prey.

That night his phone, E-Pass transponder, and keys were stolen from him while inside the auditorium. He had to call a towing truck to come get into his vehicle. He was alone for a while as he waited for help to arrive. He realized he had a spare key inside his SUV and made it home two hours later. I continued to work with CHADD with Light and Sound for several months.

A month later, the weekend before Thanksgiving, we were driving to Tampa to the Congress for Enlightenment. CHADD was very tired, but he still had to get lunch and drop off my car before the convention started. I fed him, then we took a shuttle to the convention.

As we drove home from the convention, I noticed that CHADD was physically on 3D—the earthly three dimensional energy level—but mentally in another dimension. He needed to lie down and rest, so I helped him into the back seat and he slept the rest of the way home.

CHADD drove to the Everglades so he could find the sand dune. Behind the sand dune was a hidden cement cross that was abandoned several years ago. He drove up the steep sand hill but was not afraid. CHADD had just put new tires on his SUV, so he knew he would be safe. The cross had scriptures written all over it, and he enjoyed going there to pray.

The Time Has Come

My entire trip back to Miami, I was thinking and evaluating everything in my life—my family, my friends, CHADD, and my beliefs. What I had learned from Pierre was amazing and frightening at the same time. I was not only living in a phys-ical world of danger but a world filled with spiritual beings that were in a constant battle. I was right in the middle of it all!

The moment that I passed through the gate in Miami, I felt the eyes on me again. My senses were on high alert. I turned on my phone and checked my voicemails, hoping that CHADD had called me while I was gone. Nothing. No word from CHADD. I got onto the tram, went and picked up my luggage, went to my vehicle, and headed home.

I got a few hours of sleep, but I felt CHADD was in extreme danger. I knew several times before he had been locked up against his will and pumped full of drugs—all with the purpose to control his mind and use his spiritual powers for the benefit of the government. They knew, by this time, that he had additional DNA where no one else did. They didn't understand why. They did know that for what-ever reason, they had to control him instead of anyone else.

I called the facility where he had been before I left for Paris to see if he was still there. He was not. I went to see Ethel for information about CHADD. She let me into the house. She was very impaired, and it was obvious that she had been drinking and had bottles of prescription drugs on her end table. She told me that CHADD was good but didn't know when she had heard from him last. The conversation was very painful for me. To see how far she had deteriorated from the first time I met her was very sad. I told her I was looking for CHADD, and she suggested I ask Edward. She told me that he was really a good man but he lost his way when he started working for the government and marrying Katherine. If anyone would know where he was, it would be Edward. I thanked her for her time and left.

I didn't want to call Katherine because I had seen the real person she was. She was a monster who would stop at nothing to keep CHADD under her thumb. I took a chance and called Edward. When he answered, he was startled to hear my voice. I had only spoken to him once when CHADD had actually died and was revived three times. When I spoke to him, at that time, he was very concerned and rushed to the hospital to see CHADD. I asked if I could meet him alone to talk about his son. He was very hesitant. He told me that he didn't feel comfortable meeting someone that had been the reason his son had been in jail several times. I pleaded with him to meet me at Tropic Park. He agreed to meet me in two hours. I went home for a short time and left my regular phone there. I picked up my "pay as you go phone" because I knew I was being monitored by triangulation of the cell phone towers with my regular phone.

My primary reason to meet in the park was because it was a public area and I felt safer being there. Edward was right on time. We walked into the middle of the park near a paved walking path. We both sat down on a bench. I began to talk. After talking for about an hour about all of the things that happened, he seemed amazed with what I was telling him. He told me it was completely different than what Katherine had told him. CHADD had told him the same things I had told him. Edward was at first irritated about everything that I had told him. The more I spoke, the more he became receptive. He said that he didn't feel like all of the things Katherine told him fit what was happening.

I told Edward that I had certain senses and that I felt that Katherine wasn't who she presented herself to be. She had a hidden agenda and that even he was not safe. When I had met her for coffee right after I had met CHADD, she had gotten up to use the restroom and left her car keys on the table. I held them for a moment and I picked up the energy that was transposed onto them. I saw images of people that resembled the men who would eventually be following us. She was speaking to others about deceiving Edward about CHADD, and CHADD's permanent imprisonment, so he would use his abilities for those in power himself.

I asked Edward to go home and look on her computer, access the computers at their government office, think about how she came into his life, and watch for those not-so-obvious behavior, actions that would be a key for him finding out the truth about her.

Edward seemed to be very startled. He then told me that he never really felt that he knew her, even in the early days when she came into his life. He knew that working in the area of government security people were very secretive. Only when Katherine was trying to get him away from Ethel did she ever put any effort into their relationship. Once they were married, she turned off the affection. He felt it was only his imagination. Thinking back, he was starting to think it was much more. For many years, he never felt their relationship was really about them.

Edward told me he didn't even know where CHADD was. Katherine had told him that he was at a friend's house in Orlando for the last two weeks. I told him that was not true. That CHADD had called me when he was driven to the government hospital for evaluation again.

Before Edward left, I gave him my temporary phone number to call me when he wanted to discuss CHADD more.

Two days later, he called and asked to meet me in the park again. As I was waiting for him, I saw the same pair of men that I had seen before. They were sitting in a car. Edward met me there, and we went to sit on the bench. Edward was very sullen.

He told me that he had access to certain files at work and found out the real story of Katherine. Their entire relationship was a sham. She too was involved in black ops that revolved around CHADD and that he found out about the government hospital where CHADD was.

He found first a published book that is a moving account of a former patient that survived years of unwanted and unwarranted confinement at the same government hospital as him. Edward found out that the doctor and cofounder of the International Human Rights Commission, a famous professor emeritus of psychiatry, is challenging his own profession to alert the American public of the potential danger in giving psychiatric drugs, which he considers poison and an ineffective approach to treating patients.

Working with journalists, the commission helped investigate and subsequently expose the fact that numerous school shooters had been under the influence of psychiatric drugs, documented to cause violence, suicide, and mania. This resulted in various state hearings, which investigated this issue bringing about an influx of national press coverage. The commission also documented numerous cases of parents being coerced, pressured, or forced to give their children psychiatric drugs as a condition of attending school, including parents charged with medical neglect, to give their children a drug documented to cause suicide and violence. The Commission for Human Rights stated, "Governments should endorse and fund non-drug treatments as an alternative to the dangerous drugs currently being used, proven to be no more effective than a placebo, and more dangerous than most street drugs."

Edward understood that the difference between a medical disease and a psychiatric disorder was that diabetes is a disease, cancer can be detected by a blood test, and heart failure can be seen in an X-ray. There is no blood test, X-ray, lab, or any medical test that can prove that mental illness is a disease. CHADD had been treated with drugs for years with the cooperation of Katherine and suffered a multitude of hospitalizations because the government wanted control! The government wanted control of CHADD because of his unique DNA activations and was afraid that he would bring enlightenment to the world as the universe carne into alignment. By having CHADD share the word of God with people, world governments would lose control. President Mundi and the ruling Cathari could not have that.

Edward told me that he must get him away from the government control before CHADD could become a puppet for evil. We drove to the new location where the government was keeping CHADD.

As we drove up to the parking lot, we passed the entrance to the hospital. Edward saw Katherine's car there. We saw her pushing his wheelchair out the front door. CHADD had his head down and was not speaking or moving. Paul, her son, was with her. Edward turned around and drove up behind her. She was startled. She and Paul tried to quickly put CHADD in the car. Edward jumped out of the car and grabbed the handles of the wheelchair. Paul went to strike him. Edward blocked his attack. Before Edward knew it, the same two men that I had seen before at one of the conventions came running out of the hospital. They started to wrestle with Edward, attempting to restrain him so Katherine and Paul could load CHADD into the car. Edward freed himself from their grasp.

He backed away from them to gain his balance for another assault. Suddenly the men that were watching us in the park just minutes earlier pulled up in front of Katherine's car, blocking her in. The two men that had been on the sidewalk fighting with Edward turned completely around to see who it was. The other two men exited their car.

A loud voice came out of the sky. "What God wants, God gets." The sky turned black and beams of light rang out. The wind began to blow strongly. Branches in the trees were bent, and then the rain started pouring down. The ensuing thunderstorm started to grow in intensity with blinding flashes of light. Hail the size of tennis balls started to fall down heavily. People were screaming and running in every direction, silhouettes fading away in the dark.

Edward, whose health was declining lately, fainted, fell, and did not survive it. But he left happy and in peace. He knew his son was saved and free now.

Katherine was struck by a ball of white light, died, and was dematerialized instantaneously—nothing was left of her body to be found.

Paul decided that from then on, he would do everything in his power to help his half brother and to never be an obstacle to his happiness and freedom anymore. He intended that day to help VIE reestablish the truth and his half brother's image that had been damaged by the control he had been on since his youngest age due to the conspiracy between dark energies in powerful places, Katherine, and the numerous mental places and hospitals he had been placed on so many times against his will, because his half brother had nothing wrong but he was too brilliant and they felt endangered by it. They feared that he was a threat to their agenda! Paul knew that the truth revealed would set CHADD free and that he deserved freedom of life, free will, happiness, and to go on with his destiny.

CHADD saw the Ruby placed on the roof that was guiding him in the dark. He saw the Dove.

He knew that they were finally free from the curse and that their destiny was at hand. He was finally reunited with Ruby.

He also remembered that he was reborn into his original par-ents when his DNA was changed during his coma.

Prophecy fulfilled.

The Keeper of the Sacred Knowledge now resides on planet earth. It is the sweet perfume of freedom that will incite you to recall your connection to the Source through your higher self, the recon-nection to the heart. It is by reconnecting to the human heart to the Divine that the planet will be saved. The heart has a magnetic resonance.

Is this just a story or our true reality?

"Toko Mononik Toe Koe Moe No Knee Oak"

Go Through This Gate
to Spiritual Awakening

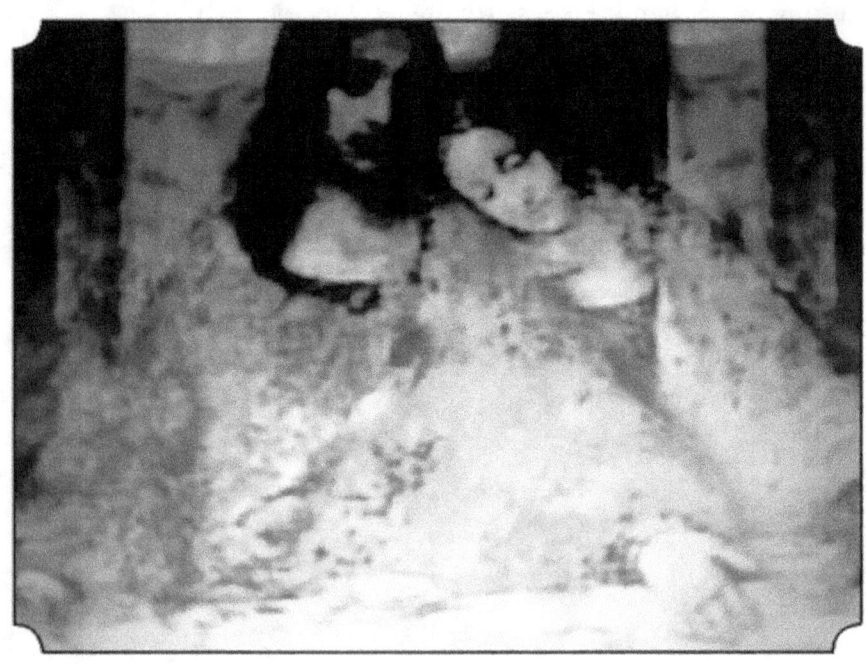

Words of VIE

The Hague, June 14, 2003

This complaint brings the International Court of Justice the greatest crimes ever committed in the course of the human history. The accused are charged with causing injury to and the death of mil-lions of people through the "business with disease" war crimes and other crimes against humanity. These crimes fall under the jurisdic-tion of the International Criminal Court.

1. The Deliberate Expansion of Disease. The following specific evidence is presented that today's most common diseases are deliberately maintained and expanded, despite the fact that these diseases could have been effectively prevented and largely eradicated saving millions of lives.

   1.1 Coronary Heart Disease...

   1.2 High Blood Pressure...

   1.3 Heart Failure...

   1.4 Irregular Heartbeat...

   1.5 Cancer. Until recently cancer has been considered a death verdict. Recent advances in natural health and cellular medicine have fundamentally changed that. For this reason too, it is a scientific fact that all cancers spread by the same mechanism, the use of collagen digesting enzymes (collagenases, metalloproteinase). The therapeutic use of natural amino acid lysine—especially together with other non-patentable micronutrients—can block these enzymes and the-ory inhibit the spread of the cancer cells. All types of cancer studied thus far respond to this therapeutic approach including breast cancer, prostate cancer, lung cancer, skin cancer, fibroblastoma, synovial can-cer and any other forms of cancer. This only reason why this break-through in medicine has not been investigated further and applied in treatment of cancer patients worldwide is the fact that these sub-stances are not patentable under the presence of treating cancer. "Chemo-therapy" toxic substances, including derivatives of mustard gas, are applied to patients. These toxic agents also destroy millions of healthy cells in the body.

1.6 Other diseases

In similar way, other degenerative, inflammatory, infectious diseases and many others of today's most common diseases only continue to exist as health problems.

Cholesterol-lowering drugs: These drugs are known to cause cancer and is currently administered to millions of patients worldwide.

Chemotherapy drugs: In fact they cause a series of severe side effects the most frequent of which is setting off new cancers.

Aspirin: Known to cause and destroy collagen and gradually increase the risk of heart attack and strokes as well as stomach ulcers and gastrointestinal bleeding...

Anti-inflammatory drugs: Many destroy connective tissue, e.g. the joints. With long- term use it is known to cause an increase of heart attacks, strokes and other diseases.

Calcium: With long-term use produces the same.

Estrogen and other hormones are known to cause cancer in more than 30% of the humans taking them. Particularly frequent forms of cancer by these drugs are hormone dependent cancer such as the cancer to the breast and the uterus.

Tranquillizers and anti-depressants cause addiction in order to increase drug sales. Including widespread diazepam (valium) is known to cause dependency and addiction. (And it gave to many suicidal thoughts!)

Drugs are synthetic molecules and therefore toxic to the human body...causing damage and gradually generating new diseases as the basis for new drugs markets.

Withholding life-saving information about non-patentable natural therapies.

Publicly discrediting non-patentable therapies.

It is a fact that we are being conditioned every day with drug ads on television, on the radio, and in practically every magazine. The major pharmacies offer flu shots. Our children are poisoned by vaccines that contain mercury a few days after birth. Several drug programs are paid by the government. Prescription drugs are the primary type of drug that is used by patients at rehabilitation centers. Medical pin centers are opened all over. Doctors and prescription drugs companies have been known to have cozy relationships.

Drug companies will send pharmaceutical reps to visit doctors and promote their product, leaving then with samples. The perks for doctors are that they can assemble panels, review drugs, and are asked to give lectures. We are in a world where we are losing more and more control over our lives and are losing our connection to God. We must open our eyes and see the light.

Ninety percent of human DNA are a portal. How can science measure it? This 90 percent has been disconnected after the fall of Atlantis!

The Door to the Divine

The Energy Ascension arrived with the Equinox of March 2013. We have been conditioned by media, the government, and the church to believe that earth will be taken over by aliens, or that we will be exterminated by nuclear holocaust, etc. Please do not buy it!

Because if you chose this path, ascension is a gateway and it brings heaven on earth. It is the beginning of a new era.

What science does not understand are the things we inherit as children and that have to do with the emotional aspects of past lives—that plays a role in aging and these aspects show up in the later years. The human body is about to go to the most alterations mentally and physically. The genetic composition of your body is changing. It is preparing us for the uplift in consciousness. If you don't understand love, feel unloved, if you have a belief that you are destined to age according to the numbers of years that you have lived, and if your heart is shut off, you will be influenced by these as it is, then a self-fulfilling prophecy, and you will age faster.

Self-worth, nutrition, and exercise play an important role.

As many have become aware, this planet is moving out of the realms of linear time. These planetary realignments are only done when specific gridlines have intersected and when the human race has demonstrated its readiness to ascend to a higher level of evolve-ment…

as the case has been in the past. Many of the physical effects you are experiencing are intentionally being initiated.

Meridian lines: Originally the meridian lines (also called acupuncture lines) in our bodies were connected to the gridlines that encircle the planet and cross at acknowledged power places such as Machu Picchu and Sedona. These grid lines were designed to continue out and connect us to a vastly large grid, tying us into the universe. This interface is a channel that facilitates our communication of energy, light, and information between large and small, macrocosm and microcosm, the universe and humankind. At one point in time, we became disconnected from these lines and lost the fullness of our inherent connection to the universe, distancing us from our previously rapid and expansive rate of evolution.

The reconnection brings in "new" axiatonal lines that reconnect us on a more powerful and evolved level lines than ever before. These lines are part of a timeless network of intelligence, a parallel dimensional system that draws the basic energy for the renewal functions of the human body. Meridian lines are reactivated, allowing for the exchange, beyond energy, of light and informing the reconnection of DNA strands and the reintegration of strings (simultaneously occurring or parallel planes of existence). Although science sees human DNA as two strands, a double helix, there are many more strands that exist within or reconnection blood, and when DNA are cleansed, blocks and emotions are released forever.

Indeed, only 3 percent of the three billion base pair genome of our DNA encodes for the construction of the physical body. Ninety percent of these DNA base pairs appear to be inactive, but it will start to quicken. There is a quickening and frequency is getting more and more quickly in energy and manifestation. Opposite forces are out to stop all spiritually aware people or people of awareness. And they are now fully starting to attack in different ways so everyone that is in any way spiritual, metaphysical, new age of the vibration.

The distance between the light and the dark side in the world is growing rapidly. The tension in the world is growing. But wouldn't we all like to be surrounded by light and love?

As the earth is purifying itself, so do we need to purify ourselves and prepare us for our own individual transition. A powerful way of doing it is by also using the Sacred Geometry to the Light and the Sound. Science has proven long ago that our bodies are geometrical designed systems. Our subconscious recognizes complex Sacred Geometrical symbols that have been used since time immemorial. Although our conscious minds will not understand, and even might think strange, Sacred Geometry has powerful effects on our mental state and also our physical body and even more powerful when added to Light and Sound or color vibrational frequency treatment.

When light reaches the crystalline structure of the cell wall, it is greatly amplified. The light radiates from the cell and naturally congregates with like cells because they share the same frequency (color) of light. These groups of cells from organs and the other structures in our body, each resonating with a specific color.

And a key aspect of the knowledge of the Templars related to Sacred Geometry, one thing that has come forth into knowledge, into reality at this time, is the connection between Sacred Geometry and modern physics and the understanding of how Sacred Geometry is used to bring forth the expression of the physical of matter, we could say.

These things are inextricably interwoven, and so the Templars gathered this knowledge and they brought it forth, particularly in those wondrous Gothic cathedrals, built under the nose of the Catholic Church when indeed they had an entirely different pur-pose, and some began to understand.

The key building created by the Templars created an ascension path, and much more knowledge about this will be brought forth in the coming times. However, that was a key purpose of the Templars. The key purpose was really to bring forth those metaphysical secrets, bring forth the knowledge of Jeshua/Jesus and Mary Magdalene. There was a great connection between the Knight Templars and Jesus's mission.

Now, understanding how Light and Sound and Sacred Geometry unlock your healing:

The geometry is a mathematic science that studies the relations between points, right and curved surface, and volume and space, and when one adds it to consciousness and the opening of the heart, it becomes Sacred Geometry forms. The forms of geometry are the mirror of our conscious; to open it allows realizing that the geometry is the base of any life on ground and in the universe.

The geometrical amplifiers used in combination with the light has the ability to balance human energy fields and contains a complex informational system that can access healing in various fields of healing using the matrix of information to explore and better understand.

This is why Light and Sound is the most all-inclusive form of all therapies as each color and sound works in harmonics interval rates and can thus be used to retune and reeducate diseased bodies, emotions, and thoughts too.

The future of healing lies in…yourself.
Light is energy.
Light is cellular communication and speaks to the cells in the body.

The human body is a beautiful matrix of light and color. We are holographic body of light waiting to be reconnected.

We all need to be reconnected with at least twelve strands of DNA. At point those that are ready and prepared will recover full power and be reconnected of two thousand strands of DNA, like before the fall of Atlantis. Geometry can enable us to remember our origins, to be helped to cure on the emotional planes, intellectual or physical. It shows that we are all interconnected and that we can perceive the various planes of conscience. By looking at it, we see various geometrical forms including five solids of Plato that are overlapping one in other. When they are studied, it is realized that nature is divisible and holographic. One finds it in many countries and as well as in Egypt in the large pyramid; besides it, ones sees also forty-seven other diagrams one behind the other, representing the chromosomes of the consciousness level toward where one moves now.

It is time that human beings bring their full cocreative power as individuals and as a society.

Awaken to your highest potential now! Humans, you must claim your mastery! Yes! You do have choice! You have been granted freedom at birth, but you are kept in slavery by the fallen angels that control the planet. Wake up! Please!

When you are reconnected, then energetic blockages are removed. Expansion of your consciousness is one of the main bene-fits, and you will simply become aware of what your purpose is and why you are incarnated at this specific point in time.

Energetic blockages are then removed, allowing embodiment of your higher self, the part of you closest to the Source, or God. Your dormant brain will start to become active, especially your pineal gland. Some of the physical benefits reported include rejuvenation of old various muscles and increase of energy. Your body will undergo a detoxification, which will bring old emotional issues to the surface to be cause disease and poison the body to be released forever.

Also, about one hundred thousand people around the world is estimated to have died of either drugs or chemicals in 2008. Drugs are not the solution.

For emotional support and on supplement of the light aroma-therapy, therapeutic essential oils and Bach flower essences will help and support you during the process.

Essential Oils Are Yesterday's Wisdom and Tomorrows Destiny

Essential oils are the oldest and some of the most powerful therapeutic agents known. They have enjoyed millennium-long his-tory of use in healing and anointing throughout the ancient world. Frankincense is used to cure every ailment from gout to a broken head. Myrrh, lotus, and sandalwood oils were widely used in ancient Egyptian purification and embalming rituals. Essential oils are some of the most concentrated natural extracts known, exerting significant antiviral, anti-inflammatory, antibacterial, hormonal, and psycho-logical effects. Essential oils have the ability to penetrate cell membranes, travel throughout the blood and tissues, and enhance electri-cal frequencies.

After using them, there is no doubt that essential oils were ordained as the medicine for mankind and will be held as the medicine of the future, the missing link of modern medicine, where allopathic and holistic medicine join together for the leap into the next century.

The planet is entering a time of great disruption and many will be shaken greatly by this. However, those who have connected to their spirituality, their spiritual paths will not need to experience this in a direct sense.

There has been a major alignment that has occurred with the solstice of 2012 and the ascension in March 2013. And yet many humans have not consciously awoken to what is unfolding.

In her message, Mother Mary reminded us of the three steps to prepare for it:

- Acknowledge your Creator: Jesus.
- Clear your negative karmic energies.

  The realization of the release of the karmic is import-ant because the playing fields have changed. The release of the karmic energies means that all debts are forgiven. All contracts are completed, and everyone is free to be fully responsible for their actions. This is the tremendous shift of consciousness if you allow it in. With this freedom comes great responsibility and great joy. You are eternally shifting, moving, and creating anew, over and over again. What a gift is the ability to continually expand. This is a process that cannot be terminated for you cannot termi-nate expansion.

- Rejuvenate your physical body: *reconnection.*

  Clearing your karmic past: by clearing your karmic past, you allow the body to return to its natural perfec-tion, because all illness and disease is simply your body's alert system to the fact that you have negative energy you need to clear. Humanity has forgotten this and all of the, particularly Western, medical system is about treating the symptoms. A process that is well aided and abetted by those pharmaceutical companies who make much money by sustaining that system.

"It is up to you to save yourself…but you cannot achieve it without help."

As we embrace the state of Divine union, *reconnec-tion*, our chakras flow as balanced, infinite spirals. The state of non-attachment allows energy to rise and center of the heart, offering connection with true peace, love, and joy.

This is brought to your attention by two gifted souls, the God Duo, blessed with special gifts from God. Their gifts adjust the body's oscillation. It removes all energetic blockages in your body to accrete the amount of light and activate your DNA and raise your vibrations before the reconnection and to access the fifth dimension. "We ask you to save your soul! You have been kept in the dark and you have been lied to. It is not what you think. There is a big battle behind the veil…technology that you are not even aware of. Are you happy with what is going on with your money, your life. You are under manipulation. You have to do your part to save your world and your children and your soul."

Here is what is written in the book of knowledge about it:

Extract from The Book of Knowledge: The Keys of Enoch by J. J. Hurtak

Key 3.1.7.9: The human evolution is preconditioned experiment within a world of happenstance relativity. Without higher evolutionary programming or direct programming by oversell intelligence, the human biological system must go back into overall flux of magnetic fields when the system is discorporate.

When man is directly programmed by oversell, he is no longer kept in biochemical slavery within a three-dimensional consciousness by the "apparent realities of the earth." The body is a grid, magnetic domain, which moves between the primary blueprint of the oversell and the pattern angles of the human organs (the axial relationship).

The lines which tie together these magnetic domains are the axiatonal lines. The axiatonal lines can exist independently but still require the governing functions of the higher evolution.

Man at this time, is being advanced to a new biological program of creation. If man has to go into further soul progression he *must* connect his axiatonal lines to oversell which is also making ascension into the next quantum level of Adam Kadmon, just as Adam Kadmon's body is making an ascension into a completely new program in our Son Universe.

Here, the Divine Father calls before Himself the unity that has been perfectly balanced between the body of the last Adam Kadmon and the spiritual-physical body of the first Adam Kadmon, before the collection of the Christ as the first and the last can offer up this eon to the Father and pass into a new eon of the living light.

The physical creation is no longer separated from the divine Ain Soph, but is restored through the Christ light penetrating the flesh and the Divine Light penetrating the overall so that both spiritual and physical bodies become one in sight of the Father. A whole species is being created at this time by the bringing together of the academic oversell—human creation which allow this spiritual-biological expression of the Christ race to be advanced to next consciousness time zone of creation.

Key 3.1.7.29: The axial lines are parts of fifth-dimensional color and sound which are used to draw from the oversell body basic energy used for the renewing function of the human evolutionary body.

Conversely, axiatonal lines operate prior to the action potential for the animation of the human species. Furthermore, they bring together the all-important tonal vibrations governing each axis and all ultrasonic activities connected with the colors of healing that relate to each tone and multiple thereof.

The axiatonal network of the Shekina controls the geometric pressure fluctuations which underline mechanisms controlling new mutations and aids in the proper conversion of the chemistry of the human light spectrum into wavelength forms of the higher evolu-tion. Through the axiatonal arrangement, both acoustical vibrations of spiritual light and sustaining love are conveyed to the human sys-tem bringing the joy and glory of the living light.

The key then opens the door for sonic vibrations (sounds and ultrasound in crystalline structure) generating gravitational light within the body.

Key 3.1.7.33: The axiatonal lines can be used for the complete regeneration of an organ and even to resurrect dead, when activated by the proper energies. This key is to be used at the time when human evolutionary molecular grids are in direct alignment with the higher evolutionary resonance grid, permitting ultrasonic pulsations to allow for direct changes within vascular bodies.

Although our scientists see human DNA as two strands, double helix, there are many more strands that exist, waiting to be recon-nected. DNA cannot be tested. It is more than chemistry; it is a field and a portal. These things are the mechanics of *spirit*.

With the reconnection blood and DNA are cleansed, blocks and emotions are released forever.

But wouldn't we all like to be surrounded by light and love? How long does it take for the organs to heal? If you are taking the proper nutrition and water, exercise and have the right healer, it could take a month or two. The organs can be healed quicker. Besides water, the air quality is important to. Other factors are toxins in the body that accumulate, the amount of plaque in the veins. The colon must be cleared…all these things must be cleared before the youth and vitality return. If you were to be only working with a few five year periods, or less, like in Atlantis, it would be quicker and easier of course.

What aging is, as far as organs are concerned, is a loss of cells, so there has to be rejuvenation of cells and it takes time, about nine to twelve months before the body demonstrates any change in the out-ward appearance. But it can be done. And you if eat enough organic greens, it will heal because the body was designed to exist on greens, fruits, and nuts. The physical body was designed to eat raw food.

Raw greens, raw berries, and nuts. Animal fat clogs up a lot in the system. The same that if you eat the right diet the body would be alkaline. It is the acidic body that is causing toxins. And if the body is not alkaline working on clearing the toxins, it will not work. Toxins will still increase.

What You Should Know about Phosphenism and the Crystal of Snow

Phosphenism develops what is truly important to an individual as a priority. It helps the best in everyone to bloom through a harmonious originality expressed by creativity. Individuals can be compared to the crystals of snow, which are all different, though all the angles that compose their patterns are sixty-degree angles, which are common to all the crystals of snow. Each crystal has its own shape and harmony though, and these correspond to the individual aspect.

Phosphenism respects the collective structure while developing individual tendencies. The method is the same for everyone: mix-ing a thought with the phosphene, but the result is completely indi-vidual. Phosphenism helps the development of the best part of the individual and the blooming of harmonious originality that is called creativity.

In 1959, a French doctor discovered and analyzed the action instigating of the light on all the cerebral functions. Its method was founded on *phosphenes*, the multicolored spots that persist in darkness.

The extraordinary one discovered of this French doctor is that mixture of thoughts to phosphene transforms luminous energy into mental energy. Phosphenes then cause the development of the memory, the intelligence, the attention, the creativity, and the intuition. The application of the method is really simple and pleasant, the progress and the results fill some fast improvement.

The child learns more quickly, retains lessons, and is more attentive in class. The effects are felt as of the first meeting. It also increases in the capacities of attention and comprehension.

In Portugal, to improve the teaching method, tests of atten-tion were made on groups of children, before and after the meetings of mixing phosphenic. Thus, it was confirmed that this faculty is better after each meeting and that, by repetition of those during a few weeks, the improvement of the attention persists between the meetings.

Specific problems like dyslexia can be corrected, as well as some learning difficulties. The students realize that the assimilation is faster and that the action is felt on comprehension. The ideas are structured better. The people who need to resume their studies after a long intel-lectual idle period will check quickly their concentration is better that they retain better, more matters and they work more quickly.

We ask you to save your soul! You have been kept in the dark and you have been lied to. It is not what you think. There is a big battle behind the veil, technology that you are not even aware of.

Are you happy with what is going on with your money, your life, your health, the violence in the world?

You are being manipulated. You have to do your part to save your world and your children and your soul!

The earth's climate is manipulated. The skies are atrociously polluted. Chemtrails, which are primarily aluminum, are released in the stratosphere to reduce the population. It forms plaque in the arteries and stops life as you accumulate aluminum. It causes neurological damage, cancer-causing effects, and even elevates the pH, which is the body acidity, and oxygen levels are extremely low. The water is becoming entirely inhabitable to the life forms that live in them, undernourished and almost spent. We are mostly water and from the ocean's salty water! Our food supplies as well as your physical bodies are contaminated with pesticides and other pollutants.

All human bodies and our water supplies have unhealthy levels pharmaceuticals and other contaminants that we have accepted as a necessary evil all in the name of progress, and let us not forget the eternal quest for long life. Our reliance on fuels, the unsafe practices of extracting these materials, and abusive consumption of other natural resources has nearly taken the life of our planet. The intentional and deliberate contamination of all our planetary resources is a major step backward in our evolution.

The global warming is also a natural occurrence, so do not be alarmed by this and there will be many areas where the oceans waters will cover new areas of land!

So many of humanity believe that they have life figured out, that they have figured out how to make life work for themselves and it doesn't work as most of people perceive it and so this is about to be shaken, shaken on many levels.

God has given all of us *free will* and *freedom*. Do not let anyone take it away from you. No human beings are and will ever be God. You have free will. You were born with free will. You were born with freedom. Reclaim your mastery. Please take action; you do not have much time left.

Life is about to be disrupted because humanity needs to be shaken up to begin to question the nature of life. It will undermine the financial base of many people who believe they have their finan-cial position sorted out, to live out their lives in comfort, and so many will begin to question what life is about.

Humanity needs to prepare as has been said many times and by Mother Mary recently.

Those things are so far from the thoughts of most of human beings that there is no space for them to hear. Those who are walking a spiritual path are most of the time considered mentally unbalanced, and if you go and start talking to others about what you understand is unfolding at the end of the cycle and beyond, they think you're even more crazy.

But those who have the true picture in place with what unfolded with the solstice of December 2012 and the reawakening of the DNA and at the March equinox of 2013, you are right, all of that is going to happen.

The end of the Mayan calendar on December 21, 2012, was a gateway to a completely different way of living and of reality.

The end of the world is an illusion!

As you become more focused, you will find that there is abun-dance for all who remain on this earth star planet. You must awaken now!

Paradise is at hand!

Important Messages from the Messenger of GOD to Humanity

It does not matter who you are. It does not matter the power that you have. It doesn't matter how important you are on earth or from which social class you are born from. Whoever you are, you are not God and you will have to pay the consequences when you will pass away and you will face him.

Life is magnificent; it is a wonderful gift and you have the freedom of choice.

Let us give the glory to God because you have now the chance to change for your eternal destiny. As a policy insurance for your soul, you can accept the bigger power of the universe. We are VIE and CHADD, the spiritual warriors of God. We have gone through many battles! And we will continue to fight to save souls. We are recognized as the warriors of Christ.

We must all take a decision. The end is near and the return is approaching. Kuan will be released, one soul will be free, he knows who he is. The diamonds are eternal and will return on Divine timing.

Following my last cry and call, it is good to have been heard and to have received a friend to continue to fight in this dimension.

You are you. Who am I? I don't understand why some men are dead and some fly to heaven. This is me. I have been on both sides of the fence. I believe that I have the answer to everything: give yourself to God and you will be saved.

During eighteen years, I have known hell, and it seems to be one life and more than the time of a life. Sometimes I feel like I want to stop, but his voice in me makes me continue.

Men seem in competition around the globe like in the Olympics, but the earth is round and it is similar to looking at a hamster turning in a wheel trying to reach God. In other words, man is running after a ghost and we go nowhere.

It is time now to come back home. The game is over. Do you know where you go when the game is over?

Sometimes we are tired of being here, but I am sure that there is a Divine reason and in consequences. I do not question the ultimate authority. This is the ultimate question no human being has to respond anything whichever connection he has with God.

I went back in this other dimension to deliver a powerful message.

As an insurance policy, give yourself to Christ now and you will have eternal life.

You can be saved like me. All you have to do is to give your life to Christ.

This means that you have to change and you have to turn your life in the good direction toward the ultimate God, our creator of the universe and of all things *now*, toward Jesus Christ.

If you are lost, you can ask yourself, is there anyone somewhere who cares and worries for me? And if you listen and pay attention, you may have heard through the news that there is one Divine being by the name of Jesus who tries to tell you something vitally important before His return.

Man is an instrument in the hands of the great and loving God. Have you ever imagined being able to see colors and dance with the souls without seeing the colors?

Reaching the zero point is to have conquered violence, sadness, depression, fear, being lost, or negativity.

Love conquers all. Love does not impose, neither impose itself, but heals.

Soul has no color but the shape of a man, the soul, is nearly liquid and has no color. Souls have no odor and cannot be touched.

Humans are in spiritual battles. Spirit has no odor, but you can sense that the spirit is here.

I have met my angel on earth at a time where my soul and my spirit were at the lowest. My angel had nourished me, made me gain weight, and bring me back to perfect health, only to pick me up, to renourish me, and get me back at what is called on earth a magnificent human being.

At a time, someone sent me on to the promised land and I have gripped with my two hands. Now I have passed the test and God has invited me home. I have finished with my mission if I choose to go back. But He has asked me to continue the spiritual battle as I am the ultimate warrior of God.

Eighteen years is like a blink of an eye, but I cannot continue alone. I am delivered, I am saved, and I can continue at least a thousand years more to fight. I will not default my God. I will battle until the end of time. I am a warrior of God battling an invisible battle that is real, that is not a creation of my brain, but of the universe against Satan. God will not be defeated because He is the ultimate warrior and I will not let my father down. I am the man that looks inside. I am gripping your hands to help you. Your will guide me toward the promised land.

No more suffering, no more battles alone, a warrior has been sent to me. This is my Father talking now and he tells you: please accept my love and understand that I am your creator, and didn't you hear that I am trying to reach you?

You can think sometime, why is my life passing by so fast? I am the Messenger of GOD, and I am here to tell you that you do not have much time left to make a decision and to choose the creator of the universe. You soul is on the line. You have to choose now. You are not given much more time. Paradise or hell?

It is at the speed of heads or tails. Do you know where you will go when the end will come?

Stop! Hello! Is it an introduction? If you do not know me, my name is CHADD and I am the Messenger of GOD. Therefore I am His voice, the speaker of my father, His messenger.

I am an energy-retracting transducer for my Dad.

I am begging you to make the right decision for your eternal soul in order to have it saved and to be with me and my family in paradise, which is something you cannot imagine with your human brain. I have seen this magnificent kingdom, and I have received the order to bring you home with me. Please do not ignore this, which could be your last chance to change and save your soul for eternity. I am asking you to not let yourself...by a false god or prophet and other negative forces that try to get you into the pit of hell, where your soul will burn for eternity.

The game is over. Is there anyone to hear me? I am trying to find you because you are lost and I am trying to find you and I am trying to save you. The Holy Spirit works hard for you. Please make the good decision now because there is no more time left.

Think about saving yourself for eternity. After that it will be too late. Please, please, please make the right decision for your soul. Save your soul!

Because the earth belongs to Satan and will burn! It is all going to burn!

What God wants, he will obtain. Whatever evil men has planted on earth, God will win that battle too. As spiritual warriors CHADD and VIE, we have been chosen to help God at a cosmic level to save souls on earth.

Can you imagine golden roads, songs of birds that relax you, distress you definitively, with a sensation of a light physic, in an orgasm that constantly froze your spirit, your body, and mind? Do not forget that you have a new body in paradise that will function every day eternally. And you will be able to walk around a lake or the ocean with Jesus, whatever you will want. The paradise is even better than what you can imagine with your human brain. In heaven, sound is ecstasy and ecstasy natural. When we all reach heaven, everyone can often hear 40 Hz of sound and it will be a sacred groove and I will walk and dance with my loved ones.

We, CHADD and VIE, are the spiritual warriors chosen by God. We are human and we are not perfect. We have been created to battle an invisible battle for the souls for the highest government of the universe. We are fighting the battle for Christ.

Is this book fact or is it fiction?

Saint Francis of Assisi Prayer

Lord, make me an instrument of your peace; where there is hatred, let me sow love; where there is injury, pardon; where there is doubt, faith; where these is despair, hope; where there is darkness, light; and where there is sadness, joy.

O Divine Master, grant that I may not so much seek to be consoled, as to be console; to be understood, as to understand; to be loved as to love; for it is in giving that we receive, it is in pardoning that we are pardoned, and it is in dying that we are born to eternal life.

Synopsis (Second Book)

In Search of the Vajra, the Key to the Universe

VIE and CHADD begin their search for the Vajra that was taken from VIE when arrested. The Vajra had been sent somewhere to be a part of an ancient pagan ritual on a solstice.

The eternally warring factions of the Cathari are exposed to the world. The Vajra is recovered by only after a divine intervention of God and his followers.

About the Author

VIE is a French American writer. Her life's purpose is to present an opportunity for expansion of awareness in the heal-ing arts of Light and Sound frequencies with her coworker CHADD.

She is the founder of the Bio Institute of Light and Sound. The purpose of the institute is to awaken new frequencies within one's being, for humanity to expand consciousness, to defragment and replace old programming with the Light and Sound frequencies of the new Divine plan, and to incorporate new harmonies in the body of the human, and through this, healing on all planes will occur.

Her work has brought healing to many and is opening up the world to a new spiritual realm and preparing all of us for the new divine plan, the ascension and beyond.

Autobiography

I was born in New Caledonia, a French island in the South Pacific. It is a tiny island in a form of a cigar and located fifty minutes in jet from Fiji Island, about two hours and thirty minutes from Australia and New Zealand.

I belong to one of the oldest aristocratic French family that came to live in the island.

My father was a very wealthy industrialist. I am the second daughter of a family of five girls.

My angels are awesome!

To keep me healthy, they make me do some yoga forms. Every day they use my hands to work on, and to clean my auric field, on my body (at night before I sleep and during my sleep too). They massage me when I am under the shower also to keep me in perfect health and shape. And of course they help and guide me during all sessions with clients. I attained my certification in reconnective healing. I am also today a chromotherapist and certified in color harmonics: frequency, Sacred Geometry, and forms.

I learned supreme science Qigong healing on all levels with Jeff Primack. I presented Light Therapy at the Seventy-Fourth Annual Conference on Light and Vision at College of Syntonic Optometry (May 2006) for my friend Juliane. I introduced the light healing therapy at the Louise Haye's I Can Do It convention in Las Vegas (May 2007).

I attended and presented the Light Therapy at the acupuncture convention in Orlando 2007, also at the Louise Haye's I Can Do It convention in Tampa (2007) and in 2009 at Body, Mind, Spirit in Tampa, Florida, and 2011 in Orlando.

I am the founder and administrator of Biostimulation Institute of Light and Sound, LLC. The mission of the institute is to present an opportunity for expansion of awareness, in the healing arts of Light and Sound frequencies with my coworker.

The purpose of the institute is awakening new frequencies within one's being for humanity to embrace the Light and Sound of creation, to expand consciousness, to defragment old program-ming, and to replace it with the Light and Sound frequencies of the new Divine plan for the ascension and space, will then be created to incorporate new harmonies in the body of the human, and through this, healing on all planes will occur. Because the language of light is cosmic light intelligence, carried in color streams of consciousness, a place where everything is possible.

But remember, there is no cure, magical formula, or therapy that can change the impossible into the possible without will and intent.

And to heal at the level of cause and symptoms and fully unlock your healing, incorrect vibration must be not only retuned, but the energy has also to be raised, and using my gifts and my knowledge may help you save time.

Since December 21, some people will find out that even sup-plement is not enough. They will benefit more from the frequency of the elixirs such as essential oils, liquid crystals, silica gel, light cou-pled with Sacred Geometry and sound healing frequency. We are holographic bodies of light.

Yes, we are holographic bodies of light and we are expansion of light. We are spirit of light in a body.

"Through the radiation of the correct colors, with the right fre-quency and the adequate Sacred Geometric form, on the reflex zones the bioenergy of the cells and the meridian's energy points can be corrected. Subsequently, the physical, emotional, and mental blockages dissolve and a sense of well-being restored."

The Bio Institute of Light and Sound is now offering its newest creation: *The Frequency of Sound*. The music contained is a sonic foundation for transformation, intended to heal, integrate, and reconnect, balancing the mind, body, and spirit while helping gifted people that are labeled with ADD, bipolar, and kids that are born with new DNA and in need of love and compassion. It's for you to enjoy as part of your everyday therapeutic routines while on your spiritual journey of life.

The Frequency of Sound is a color vibrational balancing fre-quency of sound imprinted of the language of the light.

E-mail:
instituteofbiostimulation@yahoo.com

Website:
https://instituteoflightansound.com

Twitter:
https://twitter.com/Lightsound4

Facebook:
https://www.facebook.com/BioInstituteOfLightAndSound

Video:
Journey to the Fifth Dimension, Orlando

YouTube channel:
Institute of light and sound leaping horizon series

Essential oils Youngliving.com my Distributor #398498 (you can sign up by calling 1-801-418-8800 and by giving my distributor number)